T0114048

ANGELS WHISPER IN MY EAR

ANGELS WHISPER IN MY EAR

Incredible Stories of Hope
and Love from the Angels

KYLE GRAY

HAY HOUSE

Carlsbad, California • New York City
London • Sydney • New Delhi

Published in the United States by: Hay House, Inc.: www.hayhouse.com®
Published in Australia by: Hay House Australia Pty. Ltd.: www.hayhouse.com.au
Published in the United Kingdom by: Hay House UK, Ltd.: www.hayhouse.co.uk
Published in India by: Hay House Publishers India: www.hayhouse.co.in

Text © Kyle Gray, 2012, 2015

A significant portion of this book was previously published in the 2012 edition of *Angels Whisper in My Ear* (Hay House, 978-1-4019-4053-9).

The moral rights of the author have been asserted.

All rights reserved. No part of this book may be reproduced by any mechanical, photographic or electronic process, or in the form of a phonographic recording; nor may it be stored in a retrieval system, transmitted or otherwise be copied for public or private use, other than for 'fair use' as brief quotations embodied in articles and reviews, without prior written permission of the publisher.

The information given in this book should not be treated as a substitute for professional medical advice; always consult a medical practitioner. Any use of information in this book is at the reader's discretion and risk. Neither the author nor the publisher can be held responsible for any loss, claim or damage arising out of the use, or misuse, of the suggestions made, the failure to take medical advice or for any material on third party websites.

A catalogue record for this book is available from the British Library.

Tradepaper ISBN: 978-1-4019-6337-8

Printed in the United States of America

To my mum, Diane,
for her absolute love and support

CONTENTS

PREFACE

Right here at the beginning I'd like to say, if this is your first angel book, welcome. If it's one of many, welcome back.

Since the first edition of this book was published, my life has changed dramatically. Having a column in a national newspaper was one thing, but having your life story and experiences published internationally definitely brings a lot of attention and responsibility. Over the last three years, I've been blessed with opportunities to share my work all around the world. I've received thousands of handwritten letters and emails of gratitude and angel experiences – it truly has been a blessing.

One of the most intriguing things about this book is the fact that many of the people who've read it have told me it almost came alive for them. Countless people have said that the inside of the book would light up in an ultraviolet blue colour as they were reading it. Others experienced goosebumps as if someone was standing beside them as they read it in bed and one lady was adamant her copy was producing feathers.

What really pleases me today is that belief in angels is growing. We live in a crazy world sometimes and we never know what's going to happen next, but knowing I never walk this path alone has really helped me and I know it's the same for so many other people.

Sharing the ideas and information I've learned about angels gives me so much pleasure. The fact is that everywhere we go, there are angels with us. Right now, as you read these words, there's a being of unconditional love gazing at you. They absolutely adore you, and every time they look at you, they love you even more.

Angels are real. They're here right now. When you choose to arrive, they'll be there with you. What I mean by that is that many of our thoughts are in the past, or the future, or in our worries, and it's when we breathe, relax and move into our skin in the here and now that we feel the presence of angels.

One thing I've learned about life is 'like attracts like'. When we think and act in certain ways, we'll experience our life on a similar level. So when it comes to wanting to experience angels in our life, we have to be an angel. Of course there are times when we'll be faced with challenges and things we can't change, but if we act with integrity, angels will absolutely lead us along our path.

I like to imagine angels as strong beings – loving and forgiving, but also knowing when to say 'yes' and 'no'. They have an energy that can be fiery but is never forceful, and they know love better than anyone I know.

Finally, as this is the second edition of my book, I'd like you to know that I've changed some content, because as I've grown, I'd like everyone else to grow too. In particular there are new insights on life purpose and experiencing signs from heaven – my prayer is that these new ideas will strengthen your connection to angels.

Namaste.

PROLOGUE

I woke up in the middle of the night. It was dark and it was quiet, but I wasn't anxious. I was only four years old, but I wasn't scared at all. How could I be when the person I loved more than anyone in the world was sitting beside me, making sure I was fine?

I adored my nana (grandmother) and I knew that she adored me too. Whenever I was frightened or upset, she'd stroke my arm until I was comforted. She'd hug me and tell me she loved me, and I always felt that everything would be fine as long as she was there.

Things had been different recently. I knew that Nana had fallen ill because she'd had to move in with us so that Mum could take care of her. My playroom had been emptied of all my things and turned into a little bedroom and living area for her. I didn't know what was wrong with her, but all of the grown-ups were very serious whenever it was discussed and I did realize that sometimes she couldn't breathe properly.

When she'd moved into my old playroom, I'd been glad; it was just next door to my room and I'd been excited about her being so nearby. I'd thought she could play with me all the time and pop in to read me bedtime stories.

It hadn't worked out like that.

Nana had had to get a wheelchair and after that she hadn't been able to go anywhere by herself. She hadn't been able to manoeuvre through the narrow doorways of our house and get from her room to mine – and her breathing had been getting worse. The week before, she'd been taken to hospital, and when we'd visited she hadn't really seemed like my nana. She'd still had on one of the fluffy bed jackets she always seemed to wear these days, but she'd been very tired and hadn't been able to do anything. She'd smiled when she'd seen me, and said, 'There's my boy!' when I'd run in to her, but we'd had to leave quite soon as she'd needed to rest.

Now I was so happy to see her. She was wearing one of those bed jackets, so I thought she must have come home and sneaked out of her room to see me. It was good that she wasn't in her wheelchair anymore and she looked so happy to be with me as she sat there on my little bed. In fact there was a strange sensation in the room – it was almost as if I could *feel* the love coming from her.

We smiled at each other and she came closer. I was so glad she'd popped through and was feeling better. I remember thinking, *There's my best friend; she'll help me get back to sleep.* I liked to be tickled at the top of my back to get to sleep, and as soon as I thought of that, Nana started doing it. I felt enveloped in her love and safer than I'd ever felt before, almost as if I knew that feeling would be there forever.

I gradually drifted off to sleep – safe, secure and happy.

The next morning, Mum came into my room to open the blinds. As the sunshine flooded in, I asked where Nana was.

Mum seemed a bit distant. She asked what I meant.

'Is she in her room?' I asked.

Mum shook her head and appeared upset.

'Is she having breakfast?'

Again she shook her head.

I had a horrible thought – what if Nana had been taken back to hospital?

Mum left the room when I asked that question.

I bounded downstairs for breakfast and asked for my nana again.

'I saw her last night,' I told Mum. 'She came into my room when I woke up and helped me get back to sleep. She must be feeling much better. I'm so glad that she isn't in her wheelchair anymore. Where is she?'

Again there was no answer. After all, what could my mum say to this little boy chatting so innocently about his beloved nana? She couldn't tell me I was talking nonsense and she couldn't tell me to be quiet. I was raised on love and kindness, and perhaps that's the reason why Mum couldn't bring herself to tell me the one thing that would have broken my heart: my wonderful nana had died the night before.

She'd never got out of hospital; she'd never come back to our house. Her spirit had just come back to check on me before she moved on.

I know now that when you pass over, before your spirit hits the light you can do a quick swoop of your family. Nana and I had a special connection and I truly believe that she came to look at me as she went to the next plane, because I was her boy. I'd woken up and felt the love, and I think I was meant to, because what Nana gave to me that night was something that stays with me to this day. I felt protected.

I felt that nothing could ever get to me. I felt invincible. It was a blessing that would change my life.

Chapter 1

GROWING AND LEARNING

The night my nana passed marked me for life. For more than life really, because I truly believe that what we experience on this earthly plane is only a small part of what we will experience throughout all of time. It affected me deeply in many ways. Not only was it a moment of loss in my young life, it was also a moment when I changed forever.

I want to take you with me as I look back on those early years, because that moment was the start of everything. While life is, in my view, a series of chances to learn, many of which are set in motion by our own choices, I also feel that there are momentous episodes that often signpost what is to come. If you will travel with me back to that world of a four-year-old boy, maybe you'll see just what was happening and how I got to where I am today.

What my nana showed me that night was a glimpse of my destiny. Since then I've learned to communicate with angels, and although I'm still young, I've come to the understanding that this is my purpose in this life. It certainly all began that night and I thank my nana for every wonderful thing that has happened to me since then. I had a really close, beautiful connection with her, and I still have, despite her no longer being here in physical form.

Agnes was my maternal grandmother; she and my mum were close too, and it was only natural that I was going to be part of that little group from the day I was born. Those strong female influences on my early years shaped me a great deal and helped me become aware of my feelings and sensitive side. Even when that sensitivity worked against me at school, I couldn't wish it away because it brought so much to my life.

Before Nana came to live with us, we lived very close to each other – we lived in a new house at the top of a hill and Nana lived in the house in which my mum had been born. It was three minutes away at most and I saw her every day. Then, when she came to live with us, although a lot of my mum's attention was focused on her, it also gave me the chance to develop a strong bond with both of them.

When I was three, I was very ill for about a year and that brought me even closer to Nana. I had Guillain-Barré syndrome, which is a disorder where the body's immune system attacks part of the peripheral nervous system – your body is basically at war with itself. It happened after I'd had a really bad cold. It started with weakness, and some pain and tingling in my legs, which got worse very quickly until one day I couldn't walk. The doctors feared the worst and thought it was meningitis at first. I still remember getting a lumbar puncture – it was one of the worst experiences of my life and I screamed non-stop. For nine months I was actually paralysed from the waist down. I spent some time in Yorkhill Hospital, the children's hospital in Glasgow, but

I was very lucky because I recovered when I was four. It's quite a rare condition – doctors think it only affects about 1 in 100,000 people – and I'm so blessed that I haven't been left with any long-term side-effects – apart from completely flat feet where the months of physical therapy didn't work!

The paralysis was what I remember most about that time, but not in a completely awful way. What does stick in my mind is that it brought even more love into my life. I used to sit on my nana's lap for hours on end and I adored that. She'd be in her wheelchair and I'd be unable to walk, so we'd be great pals. I loved her very much.

I have lots of good memories of before that time too. Nana always carried a handbag, no matter what, and whatever you wanted, she'd have it in there. One day I was in the back of our car with her while Mum and Dad were collecting a clock from somewhere. I mentioned that I was hungry and she pulled a block of wax-covered cheese and a knife out of the handbag! That was typical of her – you never knew what was coming out of that bag. I call that type of cheese 'Nana's cheese' to this day, as she always seemed to have some available as if it was the most natural thing in the world!

I couldn't bear the thought of Nana being alone without me, so I used to leave toys with her to keep her company. My favourite toys were little plastic monsters and I'd always make sure she had a few of those beside her when I left.

Memories of those times are still so strong – watching the film *Fantasia* together, cuddling up on her wheelchair, eating hard-boiled sweets... I wasn't the first or last small boy in the world to adore his granny, and I bet there will be plenty of people reading this who recognize just what I mean when I say we were the centre of each other's world.

It's no wonder that she continued to play such a part in my life after passing over. Every time she saw me, she'd cry, 'There's my boy!' and I'd go running towards her and we'd hug as if we hadn't seen each other for months. In the summer, when Nana and her neighbours would sit outside together having a chat and the other old women would say, 'Here's Kyle, here's my boy!', Nana would get really cross. 'No, no, no!' she'd shout. 'He's *my* boy!'

One of my fondest memories of her is her love of bric-a-brac – she'd go into any shop and find some random object that she'd announce to be 'treasure' and be delighted with. That's very attractive to a child, as they spend so much time thinking that rubbish is brilliant too, so Nana and I bonded a lot over her finds and got equally excited about the things she'd uncover when she was out on her travels.

However, as time passed, all of these little parts of her personality faded. She couldn't go out on her own, so she didn't have the freedom to go on her searches for things. She couldn't even pop down to the shops to buy a bag of sweets. I know that everyone reading this will recognize the little sadnesses that come when a life on this plane is nearing its close. At that time I was too young to realize that this point of a person's earthly life is only a passing stage, but I now know that pain, loss, suffering and ageing are only moments on our journey and they give us the chance to move towards the next stage. With the help of angels, we can all find comfort in this knowledge, and I was extremely blessed to be given some of that precious comfort on the night my beloved nana passed over.

Nana was ill with end-stage emphysema for a while before she passed. She was on oxygen, her feet and legs were badly swollen and she could barely move. She always had a blanket over her legs and was obviously in pain, but even when she was really unwell I still remembered when she was different from that. She was such a cool person.

As time went on, my mum filled me in on more of the details of her passing. Nana had died the night I'd seen her; Mum had been with her at the hospital when she passed. By the time I got up in the morning, Mum had been up all night, desperately upset and not knowing what to do. She couldn't work out whether to tell me or not, but given that I was so young had decided to wait for it to come up naturally rather than force the loss onto me as soon as I got up that morning. She and Dad had decided to take me out for lunch later that day and break the news then.

We went to one of those generic family food-type places and sat together. After we'd ordered, Mum took my hand.

'Kyle,' she said, 'this is very important. I've got something sad to tell you. Nana's gone to heaven.'

I couldn't understand that at all. I had a basic notion of what heaven meant, but I thought that people had to die to get there.

'No, she hasn't,' I told Mum. 'I saw her last night.'

'That must have been a dream,' my mum told me, giving me a cuddle, 'because Nana's gone.'

That didn't make sense, but I trusted Mum. I knew she wouldn't lie to me.

'Does that mean I'll never see her again?' I asked, tears welling up in my eyes.

'I'm afraid so,' said Mum, getting upset too.

'But I want to!' I cried. 'I want to see Nana again!'

'I know,' she replied. 'I want to see her again too, Kyle, but we can't. We just can't. She's gone to heaven. She's gone now, Kyle. I'm so sorry.'

I couldn't make sense of it. Nana had been in my bedroom the night before, stroking me and looking healthier than she had for months, and yet now I was told that she'd gone forever. What was going on?

It was a horrible time. Although children process death very differently from adults and can move from one emotion to the next almost seamlessly, I felt an emptiness inside which wouldn't go away. Would I have felt better if I'd known then what I know now? Yes, absolutely.

Explaining the Afterlife

When I was young I learned that all good people went to heaven. That was a comforting and loving belief, and it brought discipline in a way, as I always worried that any naughty deeds might mean I wouldn't go to heaven! In our culture, though, many people learn from an early age that death is something to be scared of. This doesn't help when we have to face the death of someone close to us, especially if we have to explain it to a child.

If you ever have to do this, don't beat about the bush: take an honest approach and children will trust you. Explain to them that our bodies are like cars. They carry us like a vehicle, but they don't last forever. But when a car gives up, it doesn't mean the journey is over.

Tell your child that the core of what we are is in our heart. When our body no longer works, the real person we are grows wings and goes to a beautiful place where we can watch over our family.

It's very easy for children to accept the concept of the afterlife, as they have amazing imagination. They'll find true comfort in the knowledge and you'll probably find they'll even see lost family members. Tell your child that their family in heaven can hear them and, if they listen closely, they might be able to hear them too. Don't be ashamed or embarrassed to talk to them about people who have passed. Children are incredibly open. They'll take comfort where it's offered, so be generous with your stories and your memories.

We hold on to what we're taught as children, so it is our responsibility as loving and caring adults to ensure that our children hold onto the good things, not the negative ones. Having a belief in the afterlife will help them overcome any fears of passing. We all have to go through this stage in our journey, so why deny your child comfort?

Also tell your child that they have a special invisible angel friend who was created to protect them in their life. If they ever lose something or are scared or worried, they can call on this special angel for help. If they just think about the angel and ask for help in their head, that angel will look after them.

Give children comfort and love whenever you can. Surround them with positive messages and encourage them to accept the spiritual side of their existence. If you do this, you'll be giving them something much more valuable than material goods – you'll be giving them peace and contentment. What more could you wish for?

Chapter 2

LOVE IS EVERYWHERE

Not long after my nana passed, my West Highland terrier, Tora, was attacked by another dog and got an infection. Tora had always been in my life and I was inconsolable at the thought that he might leave me too.

When he did pass, I started to hear strange noises at night and believed it was Tora calling for my help. I was very upset by that, but things got worse when the sounds seemed to congregate in my room. There were deep grumbling noises which terrified me. There were gasps and choking sounds. It all sounded so scary and so threatening and I just couldn't process what was happening. I know now that Tora was just trying to send me a message and there was nothing to be scared of, but these experiences were traumatic for a four-year-old boy.

Then I started to see images – outlines of people and energy moving around – even in a completely dark room. I can still do that, but it doesn't bother me now that I know what's happening. Then, I was completely bewildered. Did other children see and hear these things? I got a *Jurassic Park* nightlight to help me, but that wasn't going to even begin to tackle what was going on! So I started sleeping in my mum's room most of the time.

Nowadays I see myself as a sponge, and that's what I was then too. I was just absorbing everything that was going on around me – some of which wasn't occurring on the earthly plane at all. Somehow, the ability to be a conduit between this world and heaven had been switched on in me. Spirits want to pass messages to this world and the passing of my nana had shown them that I was capable of receiving messages, so now they all wanted to come through with them. The fact that I was only four years old was irrelevant, as spirits don't see earthly ages in the same way as we do. To them, I was just a human on this plane who could join the many others who were passing messages between the worlds.

There's a difference between angels and spirits which I was clearly not aware of back then. Angels are divine spiritual beings created by the universe (which some people may call God) to guide us on Earth. I believe they are pre-human and have watched over our existence from the beginning of time. Only a few angels have walked the Earth; most have remained in spirit form. Angels are pure love. They are divine role models for us and they cannot judge us. They all have distinctive features, but they don't have human personalities.

Spirits, on the other hand, are the souls of our departed friends and loved ones. They are humans and animals who have left their physical shell and returned home to heaven. Spirits do have human personalities. If you were fiery on Earth, then you'll be fiery in heaven. If you were tight-lipped and unemotional on Earth, you'll be the same in heaven. When we return to spirit, we do, however, lose our ability to judge, control and be angry. Our true essence of love surrounds us again, and when we truly are love, we can't even hurt a fly!

I'm often asked whether our deceased loved ones can become our angels. Although it's a lovely thought, I'm sorry to say that they can't, because they are different forms of being.

One particular angel you will all know will be Archangel Michael, who has a fiery and strong approach to life. He takes no nonsense but always approaches things in a loving way. His appearance is strikingly beautiful: he is about 12 feet tall, has long locks of blond and silvery hair and wears armour of platinum, crystal and gold. His eyes are blue but have a burning fire in them. Often he carries a sword that is made of fire too, but this is nothing like you've seen before, as the flames are almost translucent.

'Archangel' comes from the Greek for 'chief angel' and archangels are a higher rank than traditional guardian angels. They are, in effect, the 'boss' angels; they oversee the rest of the guardian angels and their purposes.

I became aware of the difference between spirits and angels very quickly once I began seeing angels, though that came later on, when I was 15. They definitely felt different and their energy was so loving that it stunned me. Their vibration is higher than that of spirits. Spirits seem to have more 'character', whereas angels have a divine connection – they are absolutely perfect in every way.

It was probably angels who showed spirit guides how to guide people through their lives and how to bring other spirits through to communicate with the living. I do have some spirit guides, but it was through angels that I developed my connection to heaven.

Angels never interfere in our lives. They won't jump out and scare us, they'll always look like light and they'll only come from a place of love. However, spirits are unpredictable and some are willing to do anything to get through to us and communicate. This is particularly true of those who haven't moved on to heaven and are stuck on this plane. I believe that was the kind that surrounded me after my spiritual sight opened up.

I'd no idea how to process what was happening to me, so it all became very muddled, mucky and dark. I now know that heaven works on a very high vibration. So, when you speak to spirits, you must tune yourself to that vibration; if you don't, what you receive back sounds quite scary, a low-level threatening mumbling which keeps going on and on. I was only four when this became the soundtrack to my life.

I told my mum that I was seeing and hearing things, but she'd no idea what to make of it. As well as being locked in her own grief since the passing of her mother, she was dealing with the breakdown of her marriage. And now she had a little boy who wouldn't sleep in his own bed and was 'imagining' things.

For a while she wondered if I had ADHD. I guess it's only natural that she didn't come up with the real answer, because it was so bizarre. Who would think that I was being visited by spirits?

When I look back on it, I can see that I went through a lot in a very short space of time. My nana died, my parents split up and I started school in the same week. That would have been traumatic enough for any four-year-old, but the fact that I had also had my first visit from heaven meant that the changes wrought at that time would be embedded in me forever. It was a heavy, emotional time.

The sounds and visions went on for years. Actually, they've never stopped, but I've learned how to deal with them. Now the whole thing is just a part of me. Even then it was strangely personal too. I remember that as I got older and heard other children talking about ghosts and scary stuff, despite the fact that I was so scared of the things that happened in the dark in my bedroom, I never connected the two. What other children spoke about at Halloween didn't seem connected to what was going on with me. I don't really know why that was, apart from what they screamed about seemed so created, so *pretend*, whereas what I felt and saw and heard was so real. I got control of it all as I grew.

All in all, I had a good childhood. My parents started splitting up when I was four, but the divorce went on a little longer. Despite this, I was loved and well looked after. We lived in Port Glasgow, on the outskirts of Glasgow, in the west of Scotland, until I was about eight, before moving to Greenock, just three miles away. I was an only child and my mum always took great pride in my appearance – I was the kid in coordinated clothes at playgroup!

I loved dancing and singing – maybe after the Guillain-Barré, I had a need to be physical. I adored the limelight and always wanted attention – my mum would say I haven't changed to this day in a lot of respects! I don't know why I wanted people to look at me so much, because one of my most embarrassing memories is of a terrible bowl haircut that I had. My family still tease me about it, but nothing could stop me – if there was a party or gathering, I'd be there putting on a performance. I was a good little dancer and would do my robot moves at the drop of a hat! I've often wondered if that in itself wasn't a sign of what was to come. If you stand up in a room or theatre filled with hundreds, even thousands, of people who are all there to see you and get messages through you, you can't exactly be a shrinking violet. Even if there's a shy side to your nature at other times, when it comes to that precise moment, you have to be able to focus and perform.

However, despite all of that, I did get teased a lot. I was very sensitive – again, this is unsurprising, as it can be a common thread for those who are spiritually aware, or who will follow that path as they get older – and although the love that existed in my home life gave me a degree of confidence, it still hurt when I was bullied or excluded at school. Even in primary school I was frequently ganged up on and left out. By the time I went to high school, I was more obviously bullied. To be honest, I was a bit of a pushover too. I didn't really stand up for myself. I wasn't aggressive and I wasn't hot-headed, although I did get upset over things very easily.

Although my parents did divorce, they were both there for me. I didn't have the traditional west of Scotland upbringing of a lot of boys. I wasn't pushed into football by my dad or taken to stand at freezing stadiums for Saturday afternoons of sectarian chanting. Instead, Dad introduced me to things like snowboarding and skiing, and both of my parents encouraged me to be myself and to see possibilities beyond the obvious. I shudder to think what would have happened if I'd been told that I needed to stop talking about what was happening or even been punished for it – how many children does that happen to?

I would urge anyone who has a child who seems sensitive to the presence of spirits or angels to open themselves up to the possibility that there are things out there that they may not have an awareness of that could have immeasurable beneficial effects on their child's life. I believe that there can be triggers in children's lives, such as the loss of a loved one, which allow spirits and angels to come through. Another way in which a child may find themselves a point of communication between the worlds is if they have a near-death experience. The innocence of their years can result in them accepting what they encounter rather than dismissing it all as many adults would. So, if your child is sensitive to other worlds, just be open and supportive – and you never know what blessings might be drawn into your life as well.

You can, of course, close the door if you wish – but I didn't know how to do that. I'm so glad about that now!

When I was 10, my mum went to a psychic party. This was for a laugh more than anything; both of her parents had passed to spirit, but she wasn't going there for a major attempt at communicating with them, it was just her equivalent of a lingerie party night out!

Mum was working as a mobile hairdresser at the time and she was late getting in that night. While she was getting ready, her friend Susan, who was hosting the evening, rang up.

'You better hurry up, Diane,' she said, 'the medium's here and she won't read for anyone until she's spoken to you.'

'What are you talking about?' Mum asked.

'Well,' said Susan, 'when she got here she said there was someone missing that she needed to talk to. We told her we were just waiting on one other person, and she said she knew that and she didn't want to be told your name as she knew exactly who you were and she was waiting for you specifically.'

Mum just thought they were winding her up and went off laughing.

When she got to Susan's house, there was a strange atmosphere as soon as she walked in. Mum had expected it to be all jokey, but the other women had obviously been a bit taken aback by the medium's insistence that they leave her alone until Mum got there.

'She's in there,' whispered Susan, pointing towards the kitchen.

As soon as Mum went in, the medium growled, '*Diane...*'

Mum was totally shocked. The woman was talking in my nana's voice! That voice was very distinctive – all the years of smoking had given Nana a very gravelly tone.

Then suddenly the medium, Gladys, moved back to speaking in her own voice, which was much lighter and younger.

'You're Diane then?' she asked.

My mum nodded.

'Well, will you hurry up and sit down because your mum wants to speak to you!'

Stunned, Mum sat down.

As soon as she'd done so, the medium said, 'There's a queue here – your mum's not the only one wanting to talk to us, is she?'

Mum was a bit bewildered by that; well, to be honest, she was bewildered by it all.

'I've got a man here who wants to thank you,' Gladys went on. 'Do you know why someone would want to thank you?'

Mum shook her head.

'Think about it. You helped someone, didn't you? You *really* helped someone, I'm being told.'

At that point, Mum felt quite faint, because she knew exactly where this was going.

'This man,' Gladys continued, 'this man who is here with me now, wants to thank you for saving his life. He's telling me that you resuscitated him in the street and he owed the rest of his years to you.'

What Gladys was saying was absolutely true. Some years earlier, as a teenager, my mum had revived a man called Hughie.

As she thought about it, she heard the medium say, 'Yes, Hughie, she knows. I've told her how grateful you are, now move out of the way and let someone else through.'

The way heaven often works is that someone who has been there for a while will connect with this world first, then open up the floodgates to let others connect. In this case, Hughie was the first and Nana was close behind him.

'It's Agnes, isn't it?' Gladys said. 'Her name is Agnes?'

Mum nodded.

'Well, I know that you don't believe in any of this, but Agnes is telling me to ask you about her blue-eyed boy.'

That was me. That was one of the things Nana had always called me. Mum was speechless.

'Your boy's seen her, you know – he's seen her since she passed.'

This was amazing stuff. From the spirit world, my nana was giving evidence to my mum, through Gladys, that she was still there, still watching over us, and that I'd indeed seen her back on the night she'd passed over. I'd told Mum all of this before, but to have confirmation from someone else took things to a completely new level for her.

'You'd better believe in all this soon,' said Gladys, 'because that one, Agnes' blue-eyed boy, will be doing exactly the same thing as me one day. He'll be travelling the world with it, though, and you'll never question what he can see and what he can hear because it will be beyond anything you've ever imagined.'

Gladys went on to say some more things about my sensitivity and about the fact that Nana was watching over me, but Mum didn't tell me for several years. She held that knowledge close and just watched out for things.

There would be plenty to see...

How to Get the Best from a Reading

Going for a private session with a medium, as my mum did that day, can be a really nerve-racking experience. However, I do have a few suggestions which will hopefully make it easier and ensure you get the best out of it if you choose to go for one.

The first thing I would do is check out who you're going to see. Ask friends or relatives if they've heard of that medium, because there's nothing better than a personal recommendation. Check their website for testimonials and even search their name online to see if there's positive feedback about their work. Most psychics have a Facebook page nowadays where people often leave feedback about readings, and there are many ways to find out whether the person you've chosen is well respected or not.

The night before you go for the reading, say: 'Thank you, angels and loved ones, for coming through in my reading.' Think of the people who you want to hear from and use affirmative prayers to get the best result possible. For example, if I wanted a good reading from someone I would say: 'Thank you, angels, Nana and Papa, for coming through with clear loving messages and insight for my life today. Thank you for giving the medium relevant information that only I can understand!'

I believe that a medium shouldn't ask you too many questions. Leave them to do the work; it's their job, after all.

Answer with 'yes' or 'no', but be willing to listen to what they have to say. If you're unsure, think first and tell them that this is the case.

If the reading is going well, you should feel that there's something spiritual going on. A feeling of love and appreciation from your angels and loved ones should fill the room to help you feel whole.

Be open-minded. The medium may speak about things you haven't thought of or don't even want to hear about. Remember that they're being divinely guided and are speaking about these matters because they feel it is important to you.

Mediums should only give positive news and predictions. If they speak about death and destruction in the future, get your money and run! If they are speaking to spirits and angels, they will only offer love and support. Predictions of death and destruction only come from the ego, and this is a sure sign of a charlatan.

A good medium will never take the money upfront and will only charge you if they get something that fits you. If I can't get something for a client, I never charge. It means I'm earning my living honestly and you can be sure you aren't being duped.

Chapter 3

HELPING AND HEALING

Everything started to come together on my 15th birthday. A family friend bought me my first angel cards then. My mum also took me to a mind, body, spirit fair that weekend so that I could choose some gifts.

Not long after that, she saw a Spiritualist meeting advertised in the paper. It was close to where we lived, and when she told me, I got very excited because the medium speaking was the one who had conducted my mother's reading all those years before. We noticed that it started in less than an hour, so we quickly got ready and made our way down.

As we arrived fairly late, the only seats that were available were two in the front row, so it was definitely a good start.

I was amazed when I saw the medium work. She gave names, dates, places, streets and loads of other factual information to the people she was reading for, describing in great detail the person she was communicating with on the other side and being incredibly accurate. It was absolutely fascinating.

During the performance I told my mum that was exactly what I was put on this Earth to do.

I was also thrilled to have the angel cards and began to ask angels to communicate with me. My initial connection with them came through meditation and prayer. I was constantly imagining my body filled with, and surrounded by, light so that I could raise my vibration to that of the angels and see them more and more.

After learning to tune in and out of the angels, I saw them everywhere, especially when I was on my own or out in nature settings. A clear mind with no distractions seemed to raise my vibration everywhere I went and it became a natural thing for me to see angels. Being able to watch them move around with their humans was the most beautiful thing. I became engrossed by them.

Once, near Loch Lomond, while staying at a friend's lodge, I had a wonderful experience, feeling angels all around me as I walked through that amazing landscape. To this day I have always felt a presence right at my shoulder, guiding me.

I started doing short angel readings for people using the angel cards. Almost from the beginning, the guidance from the angels was so clear. The things I picked up on were just so intense and direct that I couldn't believe it – and nor could other people. It was all very exciting for such a young lad!

I took my angel cards into school and maybe used them when I shouldn't have. I remember giving my sports teacher a message one time when I purposely 'forgot my kit'. She seemed really tired and her aura was faded looking. I remember saying, 'Mrs H., I know you're feeling down and emotional right now, but you have a guardian angel who wants you to know they're by your side. The nightmares you are having are because you're constantly worrying about everything. You need to focus less on your fears and more your desires!'

Her eyes filled up with tears and she said, 'I heard you were into this psychic stuff, but I had no idea of what you could do, Kyle. I must tell you that my nightmares have been terrifying me and I'm so grateful to know that I can get through this.'

I became the teacher's pet after that message!

When I work with angel cards, I place them out, ask the person to put their energy into them by placing their hand on top of them and then ask them to think about anyone they have in heaven and anything they'd like the angels to shed light on.

I always like to give a 'personality and present feelings' reading first, as I'm keen to ensure that a person is given proof before I give them the communication the angels truly wish to pass on. Without this proof, some people may dismiss the information or advice they are given, which is why I believe it's important to provide a framework for the reading.

It isn't always necessary to have the person sitting in front of you, though. When I first started out, my mother was working at Glasgow airport and one of her colleagues was talking about going for a reading because a family member had just passed away and she really wanted to hear from him. My mum said, 'Get my Kyle to read for you – he's needing his practice.'

I'd never met the woman before; all I knew was her name was Carol and she worked at the airport. She lived quite far from me and I thought I could try speaking to her over the phone.

Carol seemed an upfront person in some ways, but I felt that she was really putting up a barrier and to be honest I don't think she thought I was going to be able to tell her anything significant or personal enough to make her believe that I had a real connection with angels and heaven. I was only 15 at the time, so that was quite understandable.

'Hello, Carol,' I said, trying to be cheery while feeling really nervous. I could feel a swirling going on inside my stomach. Nevertheless, I was excited at the prospect of proving myself. I told her that I knew she'd lost someone close to her but I didn't know any details. She made it clear that she hadn't told my mother who'd passed away, because she wanted to see if I could get in contact with them myself.

I tuned into Carol's vibe and asked in my mind to speak to her angels and anyone in the spirit world who was connected to her. I shuffled my cards and laid them out.

At that point I felt Carol's guardian angel come to me, saying that there was a great deal of upheaval in her life and that people were arguing over a man's passing. I felt that they were after what he'd left behind but no one had bothered to contact him when he was alive.

Surprised, Carol confirmed that this was all true.

The angels then brought in the spirit of the man and I could feel him around her. I said to my angels, 'Can I speak to him?' They replied, 'Yes,' and helped me form a connection with him. I said, 'Who are you?' and he replied, 'George.'

Carol was in complete shock at this point, as it was indeed her Uncle George who had just gone to heaven.

George told me that he wanted to thank Carol for everything she'd done for him. He wanted her to know how grateful he was that she'd made sure he was looked after and wasn't put in a nursing home.

There was a great deal of healing and release of emotion in the reading. Carol was also guided in her existing relationships and the angels encouraged a need for communication with her current partner.

Tuning In

I always call making a connection with angels 'tuning in'. When you begin working with angels, it is best to get into a routine of tuning in and also 'tuning out' afterwards. I always make sure I'm tuned out when I finish work and especially when I go to bed.

As you may already know, your body has an energy system called chakras. *Chakra* is a Sanskrit word that means 'wheel' and refers to an energy centre in your body. There are seven main centres: at the base of your spine, in your sacral area and at your solar plexus, heart, throat, brow (sometimes called the third eye) and crown. There are two particular chakras I focus on when doing this work – the heart and the brow.

When I tune in, I surround myself in light and open my brow and heart chakras. When I open my brow, it allows me to see clearly or use 'clairvoyance'. When I open my heart, it allows me to feel the loving direction of angels.

All you have to do to tune in is:

Visualize yourself surrounded by a beautiful white light of protection.

Welcome angels in with a prayer such as: 'Thank you, angels, for being with me now and assisting me to channel your love.'

Imagine a beautiful lilac-coloured rose opening up in between your eyebrows.

Imagine a loving pink rose opening up at your heart centre.

Once you have done this, imagine white light coming from your ears. This is a symbol of hearing the loving direction of the angels (clairaudience).

Either keep your eyes closed or open them, whichever you prefer, and say: 'What is it I need to know?' When I do this, I often see pictures or hear words coming into my head, either spoken by my inner voice or that of someone else.

If you haven't received anything after trying this, take a deep breath into your solar plexus and imagine something beautiful. As you breathe out, something will come into your mind.

It's best to write down all you see, hear and feel.

You can also ask questions of your angels. To make things easier, begin with 'yes' or 'no' questions. As you strengthen your connection, longer answers will come through.

You can also try this with a friend. They too can ask you 'yes' or 'no' questions to begin with. Trust what comes into your head afterwards.

When you feel you've finished, reverse the process. Close the rose at your heart and the rose at your brow.

Say, 'Thank you, angels, for all that was received. Please ensure any energy left around me is sent back to the universe for healing. And so it is.'

I always encourage people who are working with angels to focus on them as a force unless working with the archangel realm. When you invite angels as a force into your life, you give permission to an angel who has expertise in your situation to help. When I speak to angels, sometimes it's just their force that speaks through me rather than one angel in particular.

Writing this book has been a strange experience in some ways – so many memories have come flooding back. That may seem an odd thing to hear from someone in his early twenties, but I've been doing this for a while and there are so many stories to tell.

My first ever message in the Spiritualist church was a real turning point. What a nerve-racking experience that was! I'd been going there for quite some time by then and every week I'd put the velvet bag containing my angel cards in the pocket of my coat to take with me. I sat with a group of wonderful older women who had adopted me and they liked to pick a card so that I could give them all a mini-reading.

Usually a visiting medium would give a demonstration of mediumship, then we'd have a break and after that everyone would retake their seats ready to see the fledgling mediums practise. However, one week was different. After the break, the president and the man running this particular church stood talking together for a while. Then the man said loud and clear, 'Would anyone like to be tested?'

The ladies I was sitting with turned to me and said excitedly, 'Kyle, this is your chance! Go on, son – go and prove to them that you have something!'

For weeks on end, these ladies had been telling the president that I'd been picking up spirits and messages and providing evidence to anyone and everyone who was interested, but she'd say I was just too young to go on the platform. However, I think her curiosity got the better of her that night and she was really eager to see if I could deliver what everyone else was talking about.

I was welcomed onto the platform to sit in a row of chairs with the rest of the fledglings. The man said to me quietly, 'OK, Kyle, what I'm going to do is ask you to clear your mind and see if you can just make a connection to something.'

I replied, full of enthusiasm, 'It's alright, I've tuned in already. I've got a link and I'm ready to work!'

I was first to speak that night. I knew I had the ability; it was just a case of standing in front of 200 people and proving it.

I remember speaking to a gentleman called Francis from the spirit world who was there to connect with his sister Elsie. He brought evidence through of his quick passing and wanted to tell his sister that he was safe and sound in heaven. I remember him talking about a woman he was with who had made her own doilies. Elsie confirmed that was another close family member.

As I was giving the message, I didn't realize I was standing with my right hand over my heart. The president said to me, 'Your body is a medium. You need to recognize everything you are doing now that you don't normally.'

Elsie then confirmed that putting a hand over the heart was something the woman who made doilies had done too. I thanked her and those in spirit.

This was my initiation and it had gone well, but I was only just beginning. Going to the Spiritualist church week in, week out helped me to get into the swing of things, though. I learned how to address an audience and how to pray openly for an audience, and the connection with my angels really strengthened.

One evening, however, I didn't have enough time to deliver a final message. It was from a man named Bob. He wanted to tell his brother that he was fine, but the church was full and I wasn't entirely sure where the recipient was. I told Bob to come back next week if he could and I felt his energy distance itself from me.

That was a late night and I had to be up first thing the next day for school, so as soon as I got home from church I jumped into bed and went to sleep.

While I was sleeping, I could hear someone screaming my name, shouting so loudly that I thought the whole world would hear. I woke up and looked to the side of my bed and there was a man standing at the same height as my top bunk. He was going slightly bald and wearing a biker jacket. In a loud, almost growling voice, he said, 'Kyle, I wanted to pass on that message.'

I got a fright and jumped out of bed and ran past him.

I said, 'Angels, why is this man in my room wanting my attention and scaring me?'

They said, 'You haven't disconnected from spirit. You've failed to tune out and you've left yourself open for any spirit to communicate.'

I asked my angels to take the spirit of the man back to the light and apologized to him because there hadn't been enough time to deliver his message. I then went through my tuning-out routine and made sure I was grounded. That was the first and last time I had that issue!

You're probably wondering why, if I had such good angels around me, they let this happen. Well, everything happens for a reason and each situation will enable us to learn something more about our life and our art. By going through that experience, I became more disciplined when dealing with the spirit world and ensured I shut down afterwards and was protected by my angels.

The early days brought a new lesson every day, and each reading taught me more and more. I quickly discovered that my talent as a medium needed a bit of refinement – I was still very young and didn't always know how to pass messages on or temper the way in which I gave them. There were so many times (most of the time really) when the communication I received from the angels related to extremely emotional or difficult things. I had to learn so much and this was perhaps the side of things I was most unprepared for. To begin with, I thought all I had to do was pass on what I was given. Like all mediums, I had to learn that actually I needed to be almost as much a counsellor and therapist as an angel whisperer.

When I was 17, I did readings in a mind, body, spirit shop in Motherwell, on the outskirts of Glasgow. It sold everything you could imagine connected to healing, Reiki, crystals and angels. I worked there every Wednesday morning and Saturday afternoon in a room which was specially set aside for the purpose. The shop was run by a wonderful woman called June Moore, but I always called her my cosmic mum!

I remember working one Saturday close to Christmas and being booked for readings all day. It was wet and windy outside, but the room I was in felt cosy and happy. It was at the back of the shop, it was filled with crystals and there were swathes of deep purple fabric draping over the ceiling which made it feel like a gypsy tent at a carnival. The table, chairs and carpet were purple to match the drapes and there were illuminated glass shelves with light reflecting off the crystals and colour therapy boxes that were on them. On top of a cabinet there was a huge amethyst cave which glinted and sparkled. There was such a feeling of calm and love in that room.

My first reading of the day was a woman called Michelle. She was in her thirties and looked as though she didn't spend much time on herself. Her hair was very short, she didn't have any make-up on and her clothes were quite functional. I wondered whether she was the sort of person who doesn't feel they deserve to make the best of themselves, but pushed the thought aside, as I always try to avoid jumping to conclusions about people.

Michelle herself was incredibly friendly and engaging. She seemed so happy to meet me and immediately was the one putting me at my ease rather than the other way about.

'June has told me wonderful things about you!' she said.

I thanked her and told her how I worked, as I do with everyone. I then moved on to speaking to both her guardian angel and the spirits surrounding her, as well as tuning into her aura. Your aura is the projection of your spiritual energy surrounding your physical body. Although the energy is subtle, you can learn to see both your own aura and the aura of others, either with the naked eye or through your 'third eye', which is your psychic ability to see. Your aura represents who you truly are and how you feel at this point in your life. The energy seems to move and change in colour all the time. The colours of the aura are a reflection of the chakras, your body's spiritual energy centres. If there's an excess of one colour it could mean there's an overload of a specific feeling, situation or emotion, whereas a deficiency of a specific colour can show what you need or desire in your life. There are different layers to the aura. I focus on the 'emotional layer', which determines what's going on in your life now.

In Michelle's case, it was all over the place. The colours were disjointed on one side but complete on the other. Instantly I could feel that the last two years of Michelle's life had been particularly difficult – and I could also see this because of the bright reds, yellows and corals on the left-hand side of her aura.

I laid my hands on the top of the cards that Michelle had impressed with her energy and I could see that she was the mother of a son. She had an ex-partner who, I thought, had custody of the child. Michelle's loneliness was overwhelming. I could feel it so strongly and it was very much connected to the loss of her son.

'Much healing is to be done today, friend,' the angels communicated. 'Michelle has come through a great deal and is now ready to take back her power. You must tell her that her father wants to come through to speak with her.'

I passed all of this on to Michelle and she said she was willing to hear from him.

Her father's spirit seemed loving, but I could feel emotion building up on my chest like a weight as I mentally communicated with the man. He was desperate to pass on a message to me through the angels.

'Tell my daughter that I'm sorry,' he began. 'Tell her that I'm sorry she followed in my footsteps. I didn't want things to turn out this way and I want her to be back in control of her own life.'

I passed it all on to Michelle, but I was intrigued. 'Why is he saying that he's sorry you followed in his footsteps?' I asked her. I would never for a second pretend that I know everything, and sometimes I need to understand why I've been given a message before I can progress to the next part of it.

Michelle looked at me, clearly emotional, for a moment. Then the words tumbled out.

'I'm just like him,' she whispered. 'He was an alcoholic and so am I. That's how I lost control of Connor. I lost my child because of drinking, just as my father lost me through his alcoholism.'

Waves of loneliness were coming off this woman and I felt so sorry about how her life had been, but I also felt great optimism because there were opportunities for things to change now that her angels were communicating with her through me.

'Angels are here with your father,' I told her, 'and they want to bring in some healing for you – would that be alright?'

Michelle nodded her agreement.

'It's really important that you let these emotions out,' I reminded her, passing a box of tissues.

She nodded again, but I knew that she was ready for healing anyway.

In my mind, I said, 'Archangel Raphael and angels, surround Michelle in healing light so that she may overcome this. Thank you, all.'

Healing light surrounded Michelle. Her father then told me how proud he was of her, as she'd now decided to remove alcohol addiction from her life and that she would succeed in doing it.

'Yes, that's it,' Michelle said, 'I'm done with all of that. I mean it – I'm going cold turkey and I'll never touch a drop again. I forgive my dad, I really do.'

She smiled and was thankful for her father's presence.

At this point the angels came back to me with a further message: 'It's important that Michelle not only forgives her father but also herself. She will have her son back in her life if she does this, but she must forgive herself now.'

Michelle admitted that she was feeling very hateful towards herself and not in a good place. Working hand in hand with her guardian angels and the healing angels, we managed to release a lot of the emotion that surrounded her.

Knowing that her dad was sorry and that he loved her very much and was watching over her from heaven was not only a comfort to Michelle but also gave her strength. With his help she was determined not to follow in his footsteps anymore. She was also determined to reclaim custody of the son she couldn't bear to live without. Working with positive thoughts towards herself and prayers to the angels, she turned her life around. A few months later, she popped into the shop to let me know how well she was doing with organizing her life and I discovered that she was indeed reunited with Connor.

I remember a lady called Grace whom I read for very early on in my career. She was a lovely woman, but was having real difficulties moving on with her life after the death of her husband of 20 years.

She was actually very sceptical. 'I'm not sure about any of this' was the first thing she told me. 'It's probably all a lot of nonsense...'

Surprisingly, I get this quite a lot. I'm never offended by it, because I feel if someone has made the effort to book a session, they clearly need something, and I am very privileged to, hopefully, be in a position to pass on a communication from the angels. I just see these people as souls who need a little more evidence before they'll take the message I have for them. They don't necessarily *not* believe; they just want to be convinced.

Grace was just like that.

'Well, let's just see, shall we?' I said as she sat down.

'If there's a message for you, you can decide whether it's nonsense or not!'

I smiled at her, but I could see that not only was she claiming to be sceptical of the whole process but she was probably thinking I was far too young to be doing this anyway. By this stage, although I was getting a reputation as an angel whisperer and people were recommending me, I could still see surprise on the faces when they saw just how young I was.

Grace didn't look impressed. She tutted as she settled herself down, but I could see a sadness in her eyes and it was obvious to anyone – medium or not – that she was hiding deep emotional pain behind her gruff exterior.

'I can promise you one thing,' I said. 'I will try my absolute hardest to provide details from spirit which will help you to accept that this is true. I won't lie. I won't dupe you. I'll be honest. If there's no message, I won't make one up – but if there is one, can you be honest with me too and take it? Please?'

I waited while she considered my words.

Finally, she nodded. 'That's fair,' she said quietly.

Grace's angels came in immediately. They told me that she was a determined lady (I could have guessed that after two minutes in her presence!) and that she tried hard to overcome any emotions in her life, as she felt they would hold her back.

There was a clear message: 'Tell her that she isn't on her own. There is a man in her life who loves her deeply.'

Immediately after these words, Grace's husband came through. He showed me his passing – which had been quick – and I could see that he'd been a very well-presented man, well-dressed, with everything he could ever have wished for in a material sense.

He wanted to express his love for his lonely wife and give her permission to begin another relationship. I passed all of this on to her and she admitted that he'd always said that if anything happened to him she shouldn't spend the rest of her life alone.

However, the angels hadn't finished with Grace. I was given a picture of her in her current job, which seemed unfulfilling and draining. She was moping about and dragging her feet, and I felt my own sense of vitality drop as I watched her. I was then given a contrasting image: I saw her in an office, which I believed was a tax office, picking up a green self-employment form. She seemed so happy and full of energy in that picture that I knew that was the best life role for her.

Grace confirmed that she had once had her own hairdressing business and had been toying with the idea of starting up again. Her main worry was whether this 'moving on' would be disrespectful to her late husband.

I passed on the advice of her angels, who emphasized that this was the path Grace should take and that it was one which her husband supported. I did what I could with the message and I said it all as considerately as I could manage.

Later I heard that she'd started up her own business again and it was doing well.

By this time, although I was working at Glasgow airport as well as doing readings, I was also doing public shows. My first ever experience speaking to an audience was at the Spiritualist church I mentioned earlier. Once I'd given that first message to the congregation, I became a 'fledgling' for some months before I found a development circle in a local psychic college.

It was through this college that I learned my real public-speaking skills, such as how to address an audience with integrity while allowing myself to be grounded and in control. This psychic college was run at the time by a medium named Margaret. She was one of the greatest teachers I could have asked for and I'll be forever grateful to her for her expertise and the way in which she ran amazing meetings where so many people came week in week out to hear messages from the other side.

Initially I was very hyper and almost out of control on the platform. Margaret helped me to slow down and bring through information from heaven in an accurate fashion. Once I'd found my feet, she took a back seat some weeks and let me host and demonstrate at the college. Through this I began building my clientele privately and also met other visiting mediums. This way I formed connections with like-minded professionals, congregations and groups who booked me to speak at their events.

A favourite 'gig' was speaking to June Moore's group, Shambhala. This was one of my first talks out of the immediate area and Margaret came with me for support. There were about 100 people present that night when I spoke about angels and gave a demonstration of mediumship. I loved it from that moment on – I absolutely loved the buzz – and I still speak to that group annually.

I'll never forget the time I was doing a show when a young man came through from heaven and I spoke to his mum in the audience.

The boy was in his late teens. He pointed out his gran and mother in the audience with a cheeky smile. One of his teeth was slightly chipped at the front and the only way I could describe him was as a lovable rogue.

His mum was very happy that I'd made a connection, but I wish she hadn't been quite so vocal when she was the one with the microphone in her hand.

'I've got your son here,' I told her. 'He's a real bundle of energy, isn't he?'

'Aye, he was a cheeky wee b— was Logan!' she blurted out.

Thankfully, the rest of the audience laughed, and I was actually quite glad of her response, as it showed me that she still thought of him in a very engaged way. It was also a good way to break the ice, given that I was immediately told by the angels that this was going to be a tricky communication.

There seemed to be a huge conspiracy about how this boy had passed away, but I knew without a shadow of a doubt that he had been murdered. I often see, feel, hear, taste and smell things which relate to what I'm being told by the angels, and this time I could see myself lying on wasteland, surrounded by grass and a fence. I felt wounded and completely out of it.

Logan's passing had been traumatic, but when he came through from heaven, he was surrounded by angels who were supporting him. All he wanted to do was tell his mum that he was sorry. He wanted her to know that he would never have chosen his life to end the way it did. He didn't want her to feel embarrassed by the choices he'd made in life and he also wanted to pass on much love to her and his granny. Despite the fact that he had made their lives miserable for so long with his drug-taking and lifestyle, he had a good heart. It was simply that the drugs had changed him.

I felt that it had been very brave of his mum to stand up and take the message, as she had already been the subject of a lot of gossip and speculation since Logan's passing; to risk that again in a public arena in front of many strangers showed great strength of character as well as a strong desire to communicate with her son, even though the message would put her in touch with the darker side of his passing yet again.

However, there was something still to be addressed. I said, 'The case hasn't been closed, has it?'

She said it had, but not in the way the family wanted.

I had to be honest about what I was getting.

'I know that drugs were involved, but I feel that Logan passed away at the hands of another person,' I told her.

As I spoke, I wondered whether I needed to be more circumspect about how I was phrasing things, but I was young and all I wanted to do was get messages over to the people who needed to hear them.

Logan's mother was swift in her reply: 'Well, you try telling the police that!'

This was a hard reading to do. It dealt with so many challenging issues on this plane – issues of drugs and bad choices, of people going astray and of the enormous hurt they can leave behind – but I did what I could. I reassured Logan's mum that there were other people involved who would be brought to justice, and I also told her how much progress Logan himself had made that evening by coming through.

By accepting the support of angels, Logan could now fully move on and release his burdens and regrets. He no longer had unfinished business on this plane and he could return to the place where only love exists – heaven.

The strong but tough woman in front of me was in tears. I realized that my straight talking had actually been exactly what she needed and if I hadn't addressed *how* Logan had died, she would have got very little out of the message.

I learned a lot that night; the biggest lesson of all was that helping someone to heal can often involve teaching them to love themselves, no matter what plane they are on.

The Importance of Loving Ourselves

Each and every single one of us has one thing in common: we want to be happy. To feel true happiness, though, we must feel loved and accepted by those around us, and to be truly loved, we must love ourselves first.

Loving ourselves is one of the most important lessons angels have for us. This is because the universe has very simple laws that we can work with to create what we want in our life. The Law of Attraction is one of them. According to this law, no matter what we believe to be true, whether good or bad, we will create it in our life. So, if we are hateful towards ourselves, the Law of Attraction will draw more of the same towards us and even our nearest and dearest will have the potential to be hateful and hurtful towards us.

This is why angels emphasize the importance of self-love.

Here's an example: if you're constantly moaning and groaning about what you don't have or how everyone is negative in your life, you'll be heard by the universe and more negative situations will be brought into your life. Similarly, if you often judge or criticize yourself, you'll probably find that the people surrounding you, even your loved ones, will also judge and criticize you.

When we truly accept and love who we are, however, the universe will reflect this in our life and everything we experience will be wonderful and loving.

Self-love isn't about looking good, nor is it about arrogance; it's about seeing and believing that you are a divine creation of the universe. You are loving, lovable and the creator of your own world. You deserve the best.

Angels teach us to love ourselves and to look after ourselves first and foremost, for when we do this, we can handle any situation much more effectively. This is their message to you:

> *My friend, you are the creator of your own life. Every thought you think and every word you say creates a wave of energy in your life. This wave is carried through your life and will affect all you are connected to. If this wave begins from a place of love, because you love and accept yourself, everything surrounding you in your life will be loving and accepting of you. If you believe that what is before you is going to be the greatest experience of your life, it will be. Choose your thoughts and beliefs wisely. The universe and angels support every decision you make.*

To increase self-love, try this:

> *Look at yourself in the mirror, directly in the eyes, and say: 'I love you. You deserve good things in your life. All that lies before you is perfect and wonderful.'*
>
> *You can also say: 'Thank you, angels, for helping me see that I am lovable and loving.'*

Go on, try it – you've nothing to lose and so much to gain!

Chapter 4

MAKING SPACE FOR THINGS TO GROW

So often angels have sent messages through me for people who need to take stock of their life and consider the path they need to take. I can appreciate this more than anything, because I too once had need of these messages when I took a break from mediumship.

By the time I was in my late teens, I'd already been in contact with the other side for some years. I loved it when I could give someone a message which would make a real difference, but I was a young man and was frustrated by the way my life seemed to be going down this path almost without me having any say in the matter.

Of course, I now know that the angels knew much better than I did what was right for me and had been guiding me along that path. However, with a head full of indecision and enthusiasm, I decided to change my direction.

I'd always loved music and after leaving my airport job I'd been attending college studying music production while doing readings on the side and DJing at a local nightclub too. The DJing was brilliant and such a buzz. So I put the psychic side to bed for a while, went back to the airport part-time and just concentrated on the music side of things, building up a local fan base as a DJ.

When I was 20, while still working on the DJing, I got a job at a local hotel and worked there for over two years. During that time I entered a DJ competition to play at the Rockness Festival on Loch Ness in the north of Scotland, won the Glasgow heats, became a runner up in the final and got to play at the festival two years in a row. The judge at the competition later booked me for gigs in many of Glasgow's famous venues, supporting acts such as Calvin Harris. I was then given a monthly residency at Glasgow School of Art, where I played to crowds of almost 1,000 people.

However, I wasn't as settled with the music as I'd thought I'd be. Something wasn't right. I didn't feel that I was free of my links with the other side; I felt as if that world was pulling me back. And I couldn't just have an interest in it, I couldn't just be a bystander, I had to be a participant! Still, I needed a message myself before I would recognize this.

One evening when I was in bed I picked up a book on angels. For the first time in many months I decided to connect with them. I visualized being surrounded by loving light as I called my angels forwards and asked them for a sign.

Totally relaxed, I picked up my book to continue reading. As I did so, a white feather fell from the book onto my chest and I was overwhelmed by a feeling of love and protection. The room was full of incredible light. It was a powerful, beautiful moment. I knew that my angels were close by and that another sign would come soon – it was as if they were calling me home. I felt so settled and peaceful that I knew it was just a matter of time before something would happen that would set me on the right path.

As I lay there, the energy around me began to rise and I could see the outline of angels filling up the room. Standing amongst them was my own guardian angel, Kamael. His energy was so strong it was astonishing. I saw him as a strong golden light about seven feet tall. The feeling of being loved and watched over from a place of love was startling. At that moment, I knew I was accepted, I knew my connection with angels was still there, and it felt as though it could actually be stronger than ever.

The next day, completely out of the blue, I received a phone call. It was from an editor at the *Scottish Sun* newspaper. I'd never done any media work before, but they wanted me to go in for an interview, and within days I'd been offered a position as a weekly columnist! It turned out that a medium I didn't even know had suggested me as a possible replacement when he couldn't fit it into his schedule. The editor had tracked me down and I just knew that this was all an indication of my way forwards.

Angels helped with the interview too. Before I met the man who would decide whether I'd be taken on, I chatted with a senior journalist, Yvonne, who quizzed me about my ideas and how I worked. She was a lovely woman with a very warm and generous spirit, and as she sat there, the spirit of a cat walked in and sat on her lap. I didn't say anything; I just made a mental note of it.

After I'd spoken to Yvonne and her boss, they said they'd be in touch and I got ready to leave. As I was doing so, though, Kamael kept prompting me to mention the cat. 'She will find it important,' he told me.

I did tell Yvonne and her response reassured me about what I'd seen and about Kamael's knowledge.

'My much-adored cat, Majika, died suddenly last month,' she said, 'and I'm still heartbroken because he was so special to me. What else did you see?'

I told her that I'd seen a lot of cat energy around her but there had also been something about toes – I felt that there was a joke about someone stubbing their toes constantly. In fact, my mind had been filled with images of toes while I'd been speaking to her!

Yvonne laughed and said, 'God, yes! Last Thursday my daughter phoned me, bursting with laughter, to tell me what my two-year-old granddaughter had said. When she'd told her, "Mummy, I bang my toe," my daughter had asked which toe and she'd replied, "My thumb toe!"'

All of this secured me the job. For a while I juggled my *Scottish Sun* column, DJing and my full-time hotel job. I absolutely loved the buzz of doing something different every day. But after a while my clientele was growing so fast I couldn't fit everything in, so in November 2011 I became a full-time angel whisperer again. Angels had clearly shown me where my future lay!

That experience has made it much easier for me to understand fully when angels have similar messages to pass to others – people such as Marie.

I met Marie a few years ago when she came to me for a reading. She was yet another sceptic. She began by telling me that she really wasn't sure about 'you people' and that she would need 'evidence' before she would believe anything that came out of the reading.

I told her my position too: 'I welcome sceptics, Marie, as long as they have an open mind and are willing to believe when the evidence *does* indeed come through.'

She still looked a little angry to be honest, but I connected with her angels very quickly. They told me immediately that her cynicism was about psychics, not about angel wisdom, which gladdened me. I don't mind if people don't believe me, but I do always want them to believe in angels or they'll never be able to access all that these wonderful creatures hold for them.

Fortunately, Marie was delighted that I could give her instant evidence of the reality of angels by passing on a message about her daughter, who was a very talented dancer. I'd known immediately that Marie was a mother and when I began to ask the angels for more information, they showed me a young girl on stage, strutting her stuff (very well!) in a show. I passed all of this on to Marie – it came with quite a lot of detail – and she said, 'Yes, that was just the other week.'

As things progressed, the angels made me aware that Marie was having a very rough time and that she actually needed advice from elsewhere – she needed a lawyer. I was given the information that her ex-husband was abusive and that he'd resorted once more to mind games and violence with Marie. I remember this all so very clearly. Kamael is very direct when it comes to this type of situation. He doesn't beat around the bush and he gives me exactly what I need to get to the heart of the matter. He told me, 'Marie is in an abusive relationship, friend. You must empower her.'

This is difficult information to pass on to anyone, particularly someone who is, really, a stranger, but angels give me such specific details about people that I know I have to share them. If I don't, then the person getting the reading might not be sure of the truth of it and therefore less likely to take the advice or the healing. It can be tricky, but I had to share what I knew with Marie.

When I did, she became much quieter. 'It's true,' she whispered. 'It's all true.'

As the reading progressed, I was sent even more details about the dark emotional pool in which Marie was living. The angels showed me that this woman who had seemed so sparky and argumentative at the start of the reading was actually fighting for survival. They told me, 'She must cut the cords that tie her to Jack.'

Marie confirmed that was the name of her abusive husband.

The angels went on to say: 'Marriage is a time when you bind yourself to another soul. The energy connected to this ceremony is holding Marie in a weaker state with this man.'

Marie revealed that although she was separated from Jack, no divorce or legal separation was in place; the angels were clearly saying that the marriage now needed to be dissolved in order to free her, on paper and then in reality, from him.

At this point, rather confusingly, they brought in the spirit of a woman who was also called Marie. They said that she was there to offer support and advice to the other Marie. The spirit Marie was what I would describe as a 'nippy sweetie' – friendly and warm, but assertive and no nonsense. It transpired that she was Marie's maternal grandmother, after whom she had been named.

Granny Marie was actually working with her granddaughter's angels to bring her healing and to help release the built-up emotions she was carrying. Disapprovingly, she told me that the young Marie still loved Jack. Nevertheless, for her own good she had to disconnect from his energy and seek legal advice to ensure that the separation was permanent.

Marie wasn't convinced that she needed legal advice, but as I passed all of this on I definitely was: the angels told me that Jack had become very dangerous, not only to others but also to himself, and that he'd tried to end his own life in the past. There was a great deal of information coming through and I was becoming increasingly aware that Jack had some mental health issues, including multiple personality disorder, which were at the root of his behavioural problems. I was shown that he'd been involved in an affair which had been the catalyst for Marie splitting up with him. However, in rejecting him, she'd reignited his fear of rejection in general. This stemmed from issues with his own father, an alcoholic who'd chosen the bottle over his family.

When all of this was given to her, Marie was incredulous. In tears, she confirmed that her ex-husband's father had indeed been an alcoholic. Now, with the detailed information from the angels, she was able to piece together the whole picture and see just what damage Jack's fears had done to his mind.

Most people want to know how I can 'see' these things and I'm more than happy to explain. Let me take a few moments to tell you just how this happened with Marie. In my mind, I saw her coming home to a flat with a white door. Her daughter, the dancer, wasn't with her. When Marie tried to open the door, she discovered that it was locked from the inside. She forced her way in and discovered her man, half-naked, with another woman. It was all very distressing to watch, but I can't think of my own reactions when I see such things, I can only follow my angels' guidance. Kamael wanted me to empower this woman and that is what I would try to do.

How did I know that there were links with Marie's father-in-law? This came from the angels telling me that she was living through some old family patterns which predated her relationship with Jack. Jack's dad himself then came through to apologize for the fact that his choices had had a big part to play in the events which were occurring in Marie's life. Due to what he'd done, and what his son had seen and grown up with, a pattern had been established which, although none of Marie's doing, was affecting her appallingly. She desperately needed the strength to break that pattern and reclaim her own life.

As I was speaking to Marie, I was also getting information from my angels – it's a three-way conversation for me! It's almost like a question and answer session in my mind; if I ask the question, I generally get the answer.

So, while Marie was sitting there, responding to what I was telling her, I was asking her angels about her situation, both to get a feel for it and to get the specifics that would allow her to believe what I was saying. I could then ask the most important question of all: *What is it that the person I am with needs to know?*

In this case, I could see that if Marie didn't seize control and assert herself, the story had the potential to take a horrific turn. I saw Marie in a lawyer's office and named the lawyers and the surnames I saw on the divorce papers. But then I saw Jack receiving the papers and turning on Marie. Rejected by his wife as he had been by his father, he unleashed fearful anger. I saw him strangling her and then I witnessed her lying on the floor struggling for breath. She had got free and called the police and was now lying there terrified as she waited for them to come to her aid.

'This man has many personalities,' the angels told me.

'That's so true!' said Marie. 'He's like another person sometimes. In fact, I think he has multiple personality disorder.'

I had to ask the angels for guidance. I'm not a counsellor or a psychiatrist – all I can do is pass on what I'm given.

'Jack is even more of a liability to himself,' they said. 'His own life is in danger.'

Marie felt this to be true, but she also felt tremendously guilty. It was at this point that we had to discuss how important it is to cut the cords that bind us to situations which drain us and are not our responsibility. Marie had to think of herself and her daughter; she had to be a mother and a woman true to herself, not try and fix everything for a man on a mission to self-destruct.

Marie and I prayed to the angels together and they offered help to cut the emotional ties to Jack, which would indeed involve consulting a lawyer to sort out the practicalities.

I took Marie through a visualization in which she saw light come over her head and wash down her whole body from head to toe. I then asked her to imagine all of her ties to this situation as nothing more than strips of ribbon surrounding her. When she had done this, I asked her to repeat: 'Thank you, angels and Archangel Michael, for cutting the cords that once bound me to the past, emotions and other people. I am free!'

As Marie did this, I saw the angels surround her in loving light. Three angels stood around her in a semi-circle, while the tall angel I know to be Archangel Michael cut the cords with his flaming sword, releasing her from the situation. Marie told me that it was as if a weight had been lifted from her shoulders.

I was amazed when, within a week, Marie called to let me know that everything had been sorted and she was ready to begin her life afresh. Jack had signed the divorce papers and checked himself into hospital. Marie had been released from her past and was ready to move on with her life.

Cutting the Cords

Cutting the cords is one of the most useful practices we can learn from the angels. As we go through life, we're often drained by other people's 'stuff'. We may also be plagued by an old pattern, old relationship or long-standing burden. When we cut the cords to a situation, we make room for angels to intervene and heal it.

Although we can do this with angels in general, Archangel Michael is often called in, as he carries a sword which can cut through any problem or issue.

We can cut the cords more than once to ensure we fully let go of something. We can also do it regularly to ensure we aren't held back by 'stuff'. I often ask angels to cut the cords around me when I go to bed to ensure that no energy from my working day remains around me.

Cutting the cords isn't too difficult if you do it right. The one thing it often can do, though, is push out any emotion you've been holding in, so before you do it, ensure that you're in a space where you feel safe and comfortable. You should be warm and have some tissues just in case you get emotional.

You could have a friend lead you through the process or even record your own voice to take yourself through it:

Sit down and relax. Ensure both of your feet are on the ground, your back is straight and supported and your hands are lying on your lap.

Closing your eyes, take three deep breaths in and out of your solar plexus.

In your mind, say: 'Thank you, angels and Archangel Michael, for being with me now. Surround me in your light so I may fearlessly release the cords that bind me to the past and unwanted energy.'

Imagine radiant white light washing over your whole being from tip to toe.

As you do this, you may want to think about some of the situations that need to be released or even state them out loud.

You may also say: 'Any situation that needs to be released, reveal yourself to me now.' In your mind, you may see a memorable situation, hear a name or place or feel an unwanted feeling.

When you have gathered up all that needs to be released, imagine those issues, feelings and people as ribbons extending from your body.

Once you have seen the ribbons surround your being, say: 'Angels and Archangel Michael, you are with me now. Thank you for cutting the cords that once bound me to the past. ***I am free. I am free. I am free.****'*

As you say this, see angels coming and surrounding you, and see the Archangel Michael using his flaming sword of energy to cut these cords. As his sword slices through them, they turn to dust. This is a sign of your freedom.

When you feel that this is done, you may want to say ***'Namaste'*** *to the angels as a thank-you gesture.*

Wiggle your fingers and toes, tap your feet and come back into the room. Make sure you drink water and have a bit of chocolate to ground yourself!

Chapter 5

THE WORLD OF ANGELS

As my experience developed, I was amazed by the world that was opening up to me. I learned something from every reading, from every person who allowed me that wonderful opportunity to connect to angels and guide them to a new empowered life. With every passing day, my knowledge of the world of angels grew and I longed to share it with others.

From the early days, I've always urged people to remember that angels are divine in character. When you're in touch with your guardian angel, it's not the same as having a chat with your Auntie Betty or the old man you always see in the supermarket on a Monday morning! Now, by that, I don't mean that you should be intimidated; what I mean is that you should bear in mind that angels aren't judgemental in any way whatsoever and they don't bear grudges.

There are seven spheres of angels, with guardian angels being the first and archangels being the second. I haven't had much to do with the remaining spheres – the worlds of the Seraphim and Cherubim, Thrones and Dominions,

Virtues, Powers and Principalities –because they play a more universal role.

The angels of light are a congregation of angels who help us light up the dark situations in our life. They are angels who provide hope, insight into our situation and an answer to our questions.

These angels are governed by Archangel Uriel, whose name means 'God's light'. I always see him as a tall and handsome angel with silky gold skin and deep blue eyes. His complexion is very pale, but he glows with light in a way I've never seen anywhere else. His voice is guiding, soothing and direct. He stands for no nonsense but does have a sense of humour.

The angels of peace are a group of angels who help us find peace and happiness in all areas of our life. They work closely with Archangel Azrael and Archangel Raguel.

Azrael's name means 'He who helps God'. He is the archangel who helps souls cross to the light and also helps heal grief. He helps us move on from a loved one's passing with the knowledge they aren't lost from our life but are with us in spirit.

Raguel's name means 'Friend of God'. He is a beautiful angel with pearly white skin and hair. His eyes are white and silver. His role is to help heal family arguments and feuds. He reminds us that only love exists and that we can overcome *anything* by remembering this.

The love of angels never ceases to amaze me. I remember very clearly a lovely lady called Betty who came to me for a reading some years ago. She was in her eighties and was with her daughter. Their focus was on Betty's husband, Hugh. The elderly man was in hospital under 24-hour supervision as he was paralysed from the neck down. His paralysis was completely unexplained and the medical staff actually thought that he might have Guillain-Barré syndrome, just as I'd had all those years ago.

The family hoped that I'd work with him, and that was really what had brought about their visit. I agreed to visit Hugh in order to perform some energy healing as well as to provide him with crystals and positive mind exercises. The family was desperate for some hope and I was happy to help. Betty was an amazing woman who was open to all spiritual learning and had even had a reading from the famous medium Helen Duncan many years before!

By this point in my career, I'd been trained in Reiki, crystal healing and colour therapy. I was registered with the Holistic Healers Association, a professional body, and I knew what I needed Hugh to do. I asked him to imagine his body was covered head to toe in white healing light. Simultaneously, I did the same, while imagining healing energy coming from the universe through my hands into Hugh as I touched him on the shoulders.

All went well on that first visit and I gave Hugh a quartz crystal for his water jug. I'd asked the angels to attune to it through its healing rays. Thankfully, the hospital staff were very open to all I was doing with Hugh – it's wonderful when people have loving minds – and they had no issues with the crystal being left there for his own use if he believed it would help.

On my next visit, a few weeks later, Hugh was very interested in what I had to say about angel healing, so I began an intensive session. He was much more upbeat than when we'd last met; although he wasn't up on his feet, he did have more mobility and, more importantly, he had hope. He and Betty were soulmates, they lived for each other, and I felt his heart was breaking at the thought of leaving her on Earth. He desperately wanted to live for her.

He asked if I could give him healing again, as he'd definitely felt the benefit last time. He also wanted to know whether there was anything he could do to increase the energy of the light. I told him to be open to any healing that might come and to invite anyone in spirit who could help to step forwards and join us.

I prayed to my angels, asking them to go to Hugh to bring him healing which would cause physical changes in his body and energy.

In psychic work, the solar plexus is the 'feeling spot'. When we feel it move, it's actually because of energy changes. Lots of people wonder what this feels like; the best way I can describe it is like this: imagine a wheel spinning. All of a sudden, it spins the other way. That's what it feels like when the energy changes in a room. It's quite amazing and thrills me every time.

This time, while the healing was taking place, angels entered the hospital room and began spreading rainbow colours all around. They painted the walls and beds in bright, beautiful healing tones and spread light across Hugh's body. The whole room looked as if someone had painted the whitewashed walls with colours and rainbows. It was a joyous vision.

The angels then said to me, 'There is a man here who would like to assist with the healing.'

I replied in my own mind, 'Please welcome him in.'

A man in spirit approached us. He was dressed in nursing scrubs and said that his name was Sam. He and the angels and I all sent colourful healing light into Hugh's body. I alone could see Sam, but Hugh said that he could see indescribable colours coming through his closed eyes. The healing was working!

I remember Hugh's words as if it was yesterday: 'I felt as if I was floating – as if I could move my arms and legs again – but the most amazing thing was all the colours I could see with my eyes closed – so bright and beautiful – and it felt as if just seeing them was helping me.'

I asked if any family member had known a person called Sam who would have worn scrubs, but no one had. I gently suggested that they retain this information, as I was sure it would make sense soon. I told them how the man appeared to me: he was in his late fifties, with salt-and-pepper hair, his face was chiselled and he had rosy cheeks. The thing I really recall was his smile – he smiled a lot!

Hugh's family was so excited. They could see that his face was full of light. To see that happiness and hope in him meant the world to them. He also kept flicking his hands and even tried to lift his leg, which was a huge achievement, although very draining for him.

A week later, I received a call from Hugh's daughter. She told me that her dad had regained some mobility in his hands – and that she also knew who Sam was. It transpired that he'd been an evening ward porter when Hugh had been admitted to hospital a year earlier; he'd passed away many months before. The family had found out who he was by mentioning what I'd seen to a sister on the ward. She'd known him instantly, as he'd been the life and soul of the ward and had never wanted to retire. He'd always kept the spirits of the patients up and had brought them all little treats every day. He'd been a lovely man who'd known everyone by name and had always gone out of his way to help. He was still doing this, showing his kindness from the other side.

Some months later, Hugh himself sadly passed and I was invited to the funeral. The night before, Hugh visited me as I fell into my dreams. He told me that he was in spirit with the angels, who were making sure he was safe in their world. I asked if there was a message he would like to pass on. He said, 'Tell my lamb chop that I'm OK.'

I fell into a deep sleep and thought no more of it.

The funeral was emotional for me, as I'd become very close to Hugh, particularly as the whole experience I'd shared with him had intensified my work with angels.

At the tea afterwards, I was approached by Betty, who clutched my arm. 'Kyle,' she said, 'please can you tell me just one thing that will let me know that Hugh is safe in the spirit world?'

In an instant, I remembered my dream and told her about the lamb chop comment.

'That was his pet name for me,' said Betty, 'and he never said it in front of anyone else.'

I told her that Hugh was with the angels and that he was safe in heaven's keep.

Hugh and Betty made a huge impression on me, and now Betty has passed too, they are together again, soulmates forever.

Everyone has to find their own way to the world of angels. A follower of my column called Felicity recently contacted me as she wanted to come on a workshop. The synchronicities that had led to her decision were just uncanny.

I had written a newspaper article on angel workshops, with contributions from experts not just from the UK but around the world. In the article, I'd mentioned my own workshop and its location, which was a shop named Heaven Scent. Felicity had seen the article and thought she might come along, but it wasn't until the next day that she'd felt the prompt to register for sure.

She was at a business meeting with a guy she knew from school. 'What is it you do now?' she asked him.

'My family designs a coating for cars called Angel Wax,' he told her.

When she replied that she loved angels, he said, 'Our slogan is, "A Scent of Heaven".'

Felicity knew this was synchronicity guiding her to come to my workshop at Heaven Scent!

On the workshop, she felt the presence of her father in spirit and also saw him in the meditation, which really made her emotional. And amongst all of that, she felt her connection to her guardian angel strengthen.

One of the workshop exercises was to give another person an angel reading. One of the other students, Aria, read for Felicity and picked up the feeling of an angel along with the spirit of a man wanting to say hello to her. His name was John and he'd passed from a heart attack. It turned out that this was her father!

I spoke about my cat, Ralph, to Felicity during one part of the workshop and she told me that was her dad's nickname!

Angelic Assistance

Angels are there for us throughout our life, even when we don't know it. Can you imagine the potential for every single one of us when we channel that love and support? Why not ask for it? And why not now?

Angels are nothing more than a thought away and can help you with anything you desire at any time. Remember, they are pure divine beings, so they won't judge you on your wishes. If you ask for help for in a selfish or superficial manner, or for things that won't add to your learning or experience, though, they may retract that help. Just remember – they know what they're doing!

I've lost count of the number of people who've asked me why I don't just demand a Ferrari or pile of diamonds from the angels! While the acquisition of material things might bring me happiness in the short term, it wouldn't be something which would bring growth to me as an individual, so wouldn't be for my higher good, which is why I have absolutely no interest in such things at all. Angels aren't going to help you because you'd like a new pair of shoes to sit in the wardrobe beside the 50 other pairs you have, nor are they going to provide you with a case of expensive champagne just because you're the sort of person who falls for labels and superficial displays. However, if, for example, you were to ask for a car to get a job you'd applied for or to ensure you could see your kids at weekends, this could be a different matter – it could be for your highest good and, as such, be more likely to bring angelic intervention.

There are also a few simple things you can do to increase the angelic assistance in your life. It all comes down to the words you say and the thoughts you think. You see, angels work with free will, so they won't intervene in your life unless you permit their assistance. They also work under the Law of Attraction, so whatever you believe and focus on will come into your life.

Angels want to help, but they find it difficult to intervene when fear surrounds your heart. If you get into the habit of almost begging for help, you're making things more difficult, because when you beg, you bring fear into the situation because you're worrying that your prayer won't be answered.

There are three main tips I can give you to help with angelic assistance:

- First: affirmative prayers. Get rid of the old routine of saying, 'Please help me,' and replace it with 'Thank you for helping me.' That's right – when you pray, thank the angels and universe for *already* delivering their assistance. That way you've detached from fear and are expecting and trusting that the help will be delivered, so the Law of Attraction will indeed bring that help to you. Remember, whatever you believe will come into your life.

- The second tip is to use creative visualization. Imagine that what you're asking or praying for is already happening. See, hear and feel every sensation which would bring the best possible outcome. This will get the Law of Attraction working in your favour and your best possible outcome will be delivered.
- The third tip is to always show gratitude. Be grateful for everything in your life. Constantly thank the universe and angels for what you have received. Counting your blessings makes room for even more of them to be delivered to you.

Chapter 6

WE CAN ALL TALK TO ANGELS

I believe that we all have the ability to communicate with angels. Every one of us is born psychic and intuitive and through development and meditation we can all learn to see our angels. I'd like to take a moment to share with you some wonderful stories where people I've worked with have discovered this for themselves.

One night I was in a house in a town close to where I live. I'd been invited there to read for a group of three friends. All of the readings went well, but I picked up that one woman was much more desperate to see her family in spirit than anyone else who was there that night.

I knew that this woman, Kate, talked to angels every day – my own angels told me so. She'd asked her angels to come closer and show themselves to her, but nothing had been happening. She was desperate to see the spirit of her mum too. Now she was losing all hope and questioning whether heaven actually existed at all.

My angels told me, 'Kate's enthusiasm is welcomed, but her lack of patience is causing her problems.'

In my mind I could see Kate on her hands and knees, praying. Over and over, she was saying: 'Mum, please show yourself to me. I want to know for myself that you're OK.'

I reported all this back to Kate – which in itself was proof of angelic existence, for otherwise how could I have known? She became very emotional. She was clouding the situation with fear – she was afraid that she was never going to see her loved ones and this was affecting the connection.

Begging for a sign, or for help, will get you absolutely nowhere; you have to *expect* help, *expect* a sign. When you're open and receptive, you're much more likely to be blessed. Longing for something isn't receptive, it's fearful, because you're actually saying that you don't believe you'll get it. There's doubt in your mind. As I mentioned earlier, fear is something which angels find very hard to penetrate, as when you're afraid you've shut yourself off and closed your mind.

I took things a step further with Kate and taught her a special visualization technique to raise her vibration. Because angels are on a higher vibration to us, the easiest way for us to connect with them is to raise our vibration through visualization. Angels are beings of light, but we have to remember that we are too. When we visualize ourselves covered in light from head to toe, we join up with the light in heaven, and that allows us to connect on a more personal basis with angels.

I talked Kate through all of this and also instructed her to say: 'I am the light, you are the light, we are the light' to her loved ones and angels. Saying this helps us to remember that we're all connected.

After Kate took this instruction, she closed her eyes, welcomed in spirit and saw her angels for the first time. They showed her, in her mind, the spirit of her mother standing between two angels in front of her. She'd been looking with her eyes open when she really needed to look within.

'Now I understand!' she told me, in tears. 'I haven't been looking properly, have I?'

Kate's words showed me how I could help others to attain the same level of connection and I found it was easy to teach other people with the same approach.

You, reader, have an angel standing with you now. You can find out what they look like and what their name is through creative visualization. Just read through these questions and you'll find the answer will come into your mind:

- *Is your angel male or female in appearance? Or sexless?*
- *What height do you think your angel is?*
- *Is there a coloured light surrounding them?*
- *Are they tall?*
- *Are they wearing anything?*
- *Do you think they have wings?*
- *If so, what are they like?*
- *What colour is their skin?*

- *What colour are their eyes?*
- *What do you think their voice would be like?*
- *What's the first name that pops into your mind when you think about your angel?*

Take note of these details, as your angel wants you to know and feel who they are so you can strengthen your connection with them.

By re-creating their image in your mind and saying their name in your prayers, you'll bring their loving energy into your life.

When I was still working at Glasgow airport, one day at break time I was joined by a young girl called Nicola. I barely knew her, but I chat to anyone and I could sense that something wasn't right anyway, so I asked her what was wrong.

Nicola was a bit reticent, so I offered to pick some angel cards for her later that day. (Everyone knew about me and my angel cards!) When I laid them out and she put her energy into them, I could see angels coming into the room, feel the energy changing with my solar plexus chakra and see wonderful light swirling around. Then one angel in particular, who seemed to be Nicola's guardian angel, said that there was an issue between Nicola and her boyfriend, Brian. Guardian angels don't always appear in great detail, but this one had a green light surrounding him, which is the colour of healing. He was tall, had bright blue eyes and was human in his features but his body seemed ethereal in green robes.

He told me that Nicola and Brian had different aims in life, that they were fiery with each other and that their communication levels were low. Nicola confirmed all of this.

The angels wanted to help Nicola acknowledge her emotional side, as she was covering everything up. I felt it was important to tell her that the angels didn't feel that this relationship was right for her in the long term and that she should be looking at other options.

Nicola was biting her tongue. She was clearly unhappy and felt this relationship wasn't getting her anywhere. At the same time, she was scared of change and didn't want to let the relationship go, not knowing what would come after it.

I said to her, 'You have the choice whether to continue to live like this or to make the change and let it go.'

The angels said that they were always there for Nicola to communicate with, but that she hadn't done so in the past, despite the fact that there was a lady waiting to speak to her.

This woman felt very much like a grandmother and like someone who had brought Nicola up as a child. Nicola confirmed that she had indeed been raised by her granny. The old lady showed an image of them making curry with mince (which I could smell and taste), which seemed trivial, but actually turned out to be one of Nicola's fondest memories.

Nicola's gran said she was so sorry that they'd never got to say goodbye to each other. That was such an intense moment. She also passed on advice to her granddaughter about her current relationship, and Nicola became very emotional. Her grandmother said that she shouldn't be scared to be on her own and she should never take any nonsense from anyone. She also told Nicola that she'd always be there for her and the communication between them would exist forever.

'Your gran is always there by your side, Nicola,' I said. 'All you have to do is talk to her mentally and she'll listen.'

Nicola said that she'd always thought about her grandmother but had never thought of asking her for help. Now she would do so frequently. I guided her in those skills.

Within weeks, Nicola was regularly communicating with her grandmother and her angels. There were more arguments between her and her boyfriend and finally, after a huge argument, they decided that the relationship wasn't meant to be.

Throughout this transitional period, Nicola put in place the belief that angels were helping her. When you have this belief in your mind, they most definitely will!

When we learn to talk to angels, miraculous things occur, but there are some stories which touch me even more deeply than others. I remember a couple of winters ago, just before Christmas, most of my clients had cancelled because of the snow. Nevertheless there were a few who could travel, so I set off to the shop where I do readings. It's an old building with no central heating, just a few plug-in radiators, so you can imagine how cold it was.

A lady called Irene had booked a session. She was in her fifties, with light, highlighted hair. When she walked in, I couldn't help but notice her huge aura, which was pink with gold flickers. It was clear to me that she'd been doing some spiritual work because of the golden colours of her aura flickering in her hair.

Irene was very open-minded, but I could tell that she was going to make me work before she would confirm anything. With her pink aura, I could see there were angels surrounding her. I was told that she'd been through a transitional time and had had a lot of weight on her shoulders. I remember seeing pink energy burst from her heart. A gold and pink angel was standing behind her, holding the top of her shoulders. I didn't see many features apart from the translucent, mesmerizing eyes.

The angels told me, 'Irene has many questions on her mind, especially about family and relationships. But before we work with this woman, we would like to say hello.'

I passed this on to Irene, who smiled.

I told her: 'They want to acknowledge the self-development work you've recently begun. There's been a lot of emotional heartache, but you are starting to heal.'

Nodding, she agreed with me.

The spirit of a woman then joined us in the room and announced herself as Margaret. Irene was confused and didn't know who she was.

'Tell her it's wee Maggie,' the angels said.

Irene gasped and began to sob, saying, 'I wasn't expecting this!'

Maggie's spirit came with a feeling that made me all warm inside. I felt a real sense of love and appreciation.

'Maggie is here to show gratitude for everything your family did for her before she passed away,' the angels said.

'Thank you,' Irene replied, overwhelmed by the message.

The angels went on to show me an image of Irene in a large office building with many people around her. They were coming and going and she seemed to be directing them. There was a sense of leadership about her.

Then I was shown her sitting on a couch with a man who seemed to be her partner. In the image they were almost turned away from each other; they couldn't look each other in the eye. Irene confirmed she had a partner of 11 years, but they didn't see eye to eye.

'He just doesn't communicate,' Irene's angel told me.

'I couldn't agree more,' Irene said.

'Many changes will take place in Irene's life and everything will be well in February next year,' the angels said to me.

Suddenly the energy changed, going gold and green around Irene.

'What's going on?' I asked mentally.

'Healing angels are here to speak about Irene's mother,' I was told.

I told Irene this, but she seemed confused. 'My mother is in good health as far as I know,' she said.

'Show and tell me her situation,' I said to the angels.

Out of nowhere, pressure came down over my chest, my breathing became restricted and my heart started racing. I asked for all of this to be taken off and it was. I then saw a cruise ship in my head.

'Is your mum on a cruise or something?' I asked Irene.

'She's supposed to be,' she answered, 'but she's gone to Lanzarote with my dad instead.'

'The angels are drawing me to pressure on her chest, so I'm going to send them to her for healing,' I went on. 'Can you bear this in mind, please?'

I thanked the angels for their healing and information and continued the reading. Irene asked me about her three grandsons. She wanted to be reassured about their health.

Immediately I heard a voice saying, 'He's not autistic!'

I told Irene and she said that it made a lot of sense. I explained that I couldn't diagnose or speak about things of a medical nature, but felt the message was for her.

'It's my grandson Rhys,' she said. 'He's three and hasn't communicated out loud to us yet, although he is talented in many other ways.'

The angel who was standing with Irene said: 'This child is a crystal child and has come to Earth with special gifts. It is important that this family is not sucked in by your world's labelling. This child will speak soon; he is waiting for the right time. He is more than capable. It is important we mention his brother. He too is special, but is mirroring his brother's personality.'

Irene confirmed that her youngest grandson was mirroring his brother by not communicating and said that the angels' message came as an enormous relief.

'What about my grandson Marc?' she asked.

When I tuned into his energy I saw myself in a wheelchair and felt restricted. The little boy had cerebral palsy. My heart poured out love for this family.

The angel said, 'Do not fear, his voice will be heard.'

I passed everything on to Irene and she left with positive prayers to try, angels to work with and the knowledge that someone was watching over her.

The reading was an emotional one for both of us and there was a huge amount of information in there.

I often find out what happens in the lives of the people I read for, because they're so amazed that the angels get things right that they let me know, but what happened with Irene blew me away. She contacted me a few months later with this message:

> *I just felt the need to update you on my reading. During the reading you told me that my mum was somewhere warm and she was experiencing chest pains. You said that you were sending her healing, which I thanked you for. I spoke to her while she was sunning herself in Lanzarote, but a few days later she confirmed that she did have bad chest pains.*
>
> *She put it down to overeating and drinking on holiday and took herself off to a local chemist and got some linctus, as she felt she had a chest infection or cold coming on. Her holiday went fine and once home she went to her doctor and got checked over. She had been treated for angina 10 years before and now felt the pains were not just over-indulgence, as they were ongoing. She hadn't had any angina medication for a decade, but her concerns were real, as she was sent to hospital where it was confirmed that she'd actually had a heart attack on holiday!*
>
> *I'm shocked, stunned and quite emotional, but she is perfectly calm. The doctors have given her medication and she has to lose weight.*

My mum has never had a reading done or attended anything of that sort, but when she called to tell me about the hospital results today she was interested in you and the fact that you knew about the chest pains. We would both like to thank you for your healing thoughts, as she is sure they helped, or things may have been worse.

This is the sort of feedback that makes everything worthwhile, but there was more:

Rhys was under investigation for 18 months and they diagnosed him as autistic during the summer. I was devastated because I felt he shouldn't be labelled. Little Marc has cerebral palsy. He had so many problems at birth that they wanted to turn off his life support. He had a massive bleed to each side of his brain and was expected to be in a vegetated state. He can communicate enough to get what he wants and make his feelings known, though. He is as sharp as a tack, knows everyone, blows kisses and is a cheeky wee monkey. You hit the nail on the head when you said his voice would be heard. I took great comfort from that.

Irene and her family are very special people and I know that angels are there for them. I'm still in touch with Irene and she is taking her spirituality to the next level. She's now a member of the Shambhala group and came to some angel workshops recently. Her family all seem to be in good health at this time.

That reading also raised the issue of crystal children, which some readers may be wondering about. It's often said that crystal children are a new breed of children who have been brought to Earth for many reasons. They are generally delivered to safe and loving families who will look after their every need. They are said to be wired differently from what we would class as 'normal' children, but they may be intelligent in ways we don't understand. They are sensitive beings who may be emotional and very psychic. They are the future-generation mediums, psychics and healers, and Irene is blessed to have a little boy like that in her family. The angels will have placed him there for a reason.

All for the Highest Good

I'm often asked if it's alright for us to pray for others or to send angels to loved ones in need, as I did with Irene's mother. This is an easy one to answer – yes! It is absolutely right to do this.

People often say: 'What if someone doesn't know about the help or can't respond because of their position?' This is indeed a relevant question. This is when 'all for the highest good' comes in handy.

'All for the highest good' means that if healing or the resolution of a situation really is required for the soul's evolution, then the angels and the universe can deliver it. It means that even if a person doesn't know how to ask for help, they can be supported by the unseen forces that surround them.

This phrase also ties into the universal Law of Grace. This amazing law teaches us that when we give blessings of love and mercy to others, we can receive them in our life too.

Working with the Law of Grace, or for the highest good, also helps us eliminate the darker times from our life, as it makes room for blessings and positive energy. Every time you think of another person and send light to their life, the Law of Grace will be ensuring that light is delivered to your life too.

I believe that praying for others can be good, but think about it: many people just hope that God will help or heal their loved ones, whether it's for the highest good or not. It has been said that if we don't say 'all for the highest good' at the end of a prayer we could be bringing unwanted karma into our life.

Here are some good ways to help yourself and others. Try saying any of these:

- *'Thank you, angels, for surrounding me and my situation in healing, all for the highest good.'*
- *'Thank you, angels, for sending healing to [their name] and their situation, all for the highest good.'*
- *'Thank you, angels, for bringing light to [their name]'s situation under the Law of Grace.'*

Wording your prayers in this way definitely ensures that your answer will come in a more direct way. Try it!

Chapter 7

FULFILLING YOUR LIFE'S PURPOSE

I've always had the belief that the universe has a plan for us all. At the same time, I've always instinctively known that we play a huge part in our own destiny. Sure we have free will and can carve out our own future – but there are some things we can't change and some paths that feel as though they were made for us.

In all honesty I didn't want to become a full-time intuitive – I wanted to follow the path of music. I seriously felt that when I found the world of club music and DJing, that was it, that was my career. And to be honest with you, it seemed cooler to say to other people that I was a DJ than to explain that I spoke to angels.

The angels themselves, and the energy that I call the universe, seemed to have a completely different plan for me though. Every time I got a little bit further with the DJing, something else would come up or there would be an obstacle of some kind.

I'd read in spiritual books and heard through spiritual teachers along the way that we all had a divine life purpose – a special and specific function in the world according to the divine plan. So I trusted that my purpose was to do the angel work instead, but also felt that the Djing could become a hobby or part-time position that I could still follow and enjoy. So I'd do readings some of the time, do my column in the *Scottish Sun* weekly and then DJ on top of it. I remember one day that I filled my diary with so much I thought I was going to collapse. I did a demonstration of mediumship and angel readings at a huge event and then went to a hotel to get changed before going on stage and DJing to over 1,000 people. When I got back to the hotel that night I was completely swamped.

I wanted to keep going with both, but the bookings for my spiritual work started to go through the roof and the DJ bookings – well, they did come, but not as frequently. Even though I loved music, it seemed there was a greater demand for the spiritual work.

There came a point where I just had to surrender. I had to let go and let God.

One thing I knew for sure: I loved making people smile and I loved seeing people enjoy themselves. Seeing someone enjoying themselves on the dance floor or crying tears of happiness during a session made me feel fulfilled and happy. It felt as though *people* were my purpose. I still didn't have it quite right, but I was on the path to understanding...

Life Purpose

It started to come to my attention that finding a life purpose was a goal for many people and if they didn't have one (that they knew about), they felt inadequate. How could I direct people to the area of expertise that was right for them?

I could pick up what their current career or career goals were. I remember a girl walking into my office one day wearing all black, but in my mind she was wearing a full red uniform and felt like an air hostess. I told her straight away that I saw her working for Virgin Atlantic Airlines – and then found out she'd just completed her training with them. Another time I just knew the girl who'd sat down on my office sofa was a journalist. That's a natural aspect of being aware on a psychic level, but it still didn't feel like life purpose reading.

I'm a student of the metaphysical text *A Course in Miracles*, which has helped me deepen my spiritual practice. 'The *Course*' as it's known amongst students of the system, is a huge book made up of a text, a workbook containing 365 daily lessons and a manual for teachers. It is a channelled work that aims to change our negative thinking patterns and create miracles in our life – a 'miracle' being a shift in perception.

Since studying the *Course* I've learned that my aim in life is always to reach, express or receive love in some way. I've come to realize that I'm an expression of love and my true purpose in life is to remember that. Even though I've had goals and still make them in my life, it's not goals or trophies I'm chasing, it's the sense of fulfilment and acceptance that comes with them. The *Course* has helped me see that if I can feel fulfilled and honour that I am enough in the eyes of my Creator, my goals will come more easily, but not only that, I will fulfil my function. So, what is that function?

Angels absolutely encourage us to make goals and reach new heights in our life. They love seeing us do well and they love seeing us grow more confident in ourselves and our ability to achieve.

But when it comes to life goals, it's important to figure out why something is a goal – is it the feeling behind the goal you want or is the achievement of the goal going to make you feel better about who you are?

Your angels want you to know that achieving your goals won't make you more beautiful, special, sacred, spiritual or connected than you already are. What they want you to realize is that you are *already* perfect, whole and complete in their eyes, and they want you to see it too. If you can see that achieving your goals doesn't determine your worth according to the universe and it doesn't determine your *self*-worth, then you're onto something.

Chasing career goals can be a destructive pattern and it's important to know that they actually have nothing to do with fulfilling your purpose. Achievements in your career are wonderful of course, but you can't let them stand in the way of being yourself.

In Lesson 61 of *A Course in Miracles* we are reminded that our function is to be the light of the world. Being the light means being completely loving, accepting and forgiving of ourselves and others. This doesn't mean we have to become a spiritual teacher, healer or yoga instructor; it does mean that wherever we are, no matter what we're doing, we can be the light, but this is a choice we must make.

As my daily meditation focused on being the light, I really studied and questioned what it meant. Light is the opposite of darkness, it's the opposite of heavy, it's serene, peaceful and, most importantly, happy. It led me down the path of trusting that our true function in life is to be *happy*.

This was a complete game-changer for me, because it helped me direct my students and clients who were desperate to find their spiritual purpose. It also helped me realize that our spiritual purpose isn't a job title or a physical thing, it's a *feeling*, and that feeling is *happiness*.

Finding Happiness in Our Career

What about our career? How does that fit in? There's no doubt that many of us are talented in certain areas and so of course that can become a part of our life purpose, but it doesn't have to define us and our sense of adequacy. I think that's one of the major reasons why I've started saying, 'Tell me who you are, not what you do,' when I meet a new person.

It's knowing that the universe sees as all as equal – knowing that the angels love us all – that takes away some of the pressure we create in our own mind. Knowing that the presence of creation loves you and me equally, and loves world leaders and activists all the same, makes it all the more beautiful. That presence of love connects us all and it desperately waits for us to realize we are an essential valve within its heart.

Knowing that you are a light and your function is to light up the world allows you to bring a sense of purpose to your daily routine. If you're at a point in your working life where you don't feel a sense of purpose or fulfilment, now is the time to change that.

I recently conducted a private session on Skype for a girl who was based in Germany. She was studying for a PhD while doing a full-time job in the corporate world. We'd met before during a seminar and she'd asked if we could discuss her life and work with the angels to improve certain elements. I love a challenge, so was keen to support her in any way I could.

During our session, Brigit expressed her concerns about her workplace. She said that she found it extremely hard and that many of her colleagues were in competition with one another. Although they were all working together to reach an objective, they'd trample one another to get ahead. As a sensitive soul and someone who was spiritually minded, Brigit found it difficult to comprehend. She wanted to know what the angels could do to help her situation and if it was time to change her job.

When the angels came in, I saw them shining in the form of bright golden lights all around her. Brigit felt them too, because she began to well up.

Instantly I had a deep inner knowing that Brigit was to continue working in her corporate job but the angels wanted her to be happy there. They said she had a 'mission' to establish appreciation within the workplace. That was one of many reasons why she'd been sent there.

I told Brigit that there were huge lessons for her there and that if she could fulfil her function to create happiness in her current space of work, that ability would move with her wherever she went. I told her that appreciation was the key and that if she called on the angels, she could work with them to create a change of energy. The reading went on and it was clear, precise and insightful – Brigit knew what she had to do.

Only six months later Brigit contacted me again, saying that she'd like a review. She had to wait for some time, due to my schedule, but when we met she was in a completely different heart and head space.

She'd followed the angels' guidance and begun to tell her colleagues what she appreciated about them. She'd held a deep appreciation for her company too. And all of a sudden the energy in the office had changed for the better. Everyone around her started to get on, and not only that, her manager even came to her and asked if she could run a weekly appreciation meeting so that the team could build a stronger bond and the office stay as positive as it had been recently. She agreed and her new adventure brought her great joy and a sense of purpose.

The good news didn't finish there. Brigit admitted her PhD hadn't been interesting her for a while, but when she'd started her appreciation practice at work, she'd had a new lease of life that had led her to focus on finishing it. She now recognized her true function was to find happiness in her life as a whole in order to see it in the places where she thought it was missing. Not only that: she was making business-consulting and relationship-building in the workplace her career.

Finding Light in Your Career

So, happiness is your purpose, and that can't be defined by your career. It's down to you and how you feel within. But it's important to allow it to radiate through your career, so your career complements this sacred journey you are on.

How can you do this? Spend more time cultivating happiness and less time thinking about changing your career or fixing what seems wrong. Angels are absolutely desperate to help you with this aspect of your life, but if you're stressed, frustrated and complaining, it's as though you're pushing away their help. If, on the other hand, you can start to find happiness in the simple things and smile in your workplace, the universe will smile back right through your life.

Through doing angel readings, I've noticed if someone has a challenging workplace situation and leaves because of it, the pattern repeats itself. When a lesson comes up, we have to learn it. Usually, we have to learn how to change ourselves – we have to *be* the change we seek rather than running away.

If you're in a workplace that doesn't feel good, it's important to figure out why that's happening and aim to be happy there rather than moving on. I've found that when you're happy and then you move, the happiness moves with you, so it's better to move on with contentment rather than seeking it. In fact it's good to get in that state before making any dramatic changes in your life. The ego self (that little voice with its own plan in your head) can tell you that if you make a change you'll be happy, but that's not always the case, because it's saying the future has the answer when in reality it's only the present that currently exists, and therefore the moment to be happy is now.

Heavenly Host

There is an archangel called Chamuel, whose name means 'He who sees God'. He is the angel who is most dedicated to the expansion of the heart. He helps us find our true love for life so that we can include it in our career and personal relationships. Chamuel is known for his special ability to direct us silently to our soulmate and to a career that complements who we are and the gifts we bring to the planet. As far as I'm concerned, he's the divine recruitment officer for both love and career.

Chamuel helps us cultivate a deep sense of self-love and appreciation so that we can truly honour what we bring to the planet. He is the archangel who masters the ruby ray – the energy that helps us reach a higher sense of love and enjoyment of our duties here on planet Earth.

Anyone can call on Chamuel for help, especially when seeking the right direction in love or career. Like all the angels, he's a multi-dimensional being who can be many places at once – he's not restricted by time and space. He'll show himself to you in a way that you'll understand, so that even though I see him looking like David Bowie, that doesn't mean you will too.

Like all the angels, Chamuel can be invoked through visualization and prayer. As he's the master of the ruby ray, I invoke him by imagining myself surrounded by a ruby light. I see this energy moving all around me, from my head to the tips of my toes, and trust it acts like a magnet, drawing

Chamuel close. Then I'll share my concerns and welcome his help.

Here is a prayer and meditation practice to help connect your function of being happy with your career, so you can have a deep sense of purpose.

'Thank you for drawing close to me at this time, Archangel Chamuel, and for guiding this aspect of my journey. I have recognized that my true function on this planet is to be happy and fulfilled and I take time to acknowledge my blessings now.'

Close your eyes and give silent thanks for the blessings you have in your life at this time. See the areas of your life where you are experiencing fulfilment. Smile throughout this practice and really honour what is special in your life.

Then say: 'Archangel Chamuel, I am now welcoming your support and direction in my function and career – I welcome your support in marrying my happiness with my daily routine. It feels so good to have a sense of purpose in life and to share my gifts and talents with the world.'

Begin to think about the gifts you have. Feel the joy you feel when you share these talents with the world. Imagine that you're sharing this joy as light throughout your whole life. See angels working with and through you, and know they're on your team.

Finish by saying: 'Thank you, angels and Archangel Chamuel, for showing me where to go in my life, what to do, whom to speak to and what to say. I am dedicated to fulfilling my function, living with purpose and sharing my light with the world. I am grateful you are with me on this incredible journey. And so it is!'

Chapter 8

A SENSE OF INNOCENCE

Children are usually more in tune with the energy of spirits and angels than adults are, because they have a sense of innocence about them. They haven't been taught to be sceptical or judgemental yet, so their minds are open to seeing the true love of angels.

I was at a huge media event for a national newspaper one day when I met two women, both of whom had their daughters with them. I read their auras and spoke to their angels, and I was particularly drawn to one of the little girls.

'There are lots of angels around you, aren't there?' I said. 'They're telling me that they've helped keep you alive.'

The girl's mother looked at me in shock and said that she couldn't believe I'd made such a perceptive and accurate comment. She asked me what else I could see.

I replied, 'There's a huge angel standing with your daughter right now. They all know that she warms the hearts of others and that's why they've made sure to keep her on this plane.'

As I talked to the woman and child, the angel told me, 'We don't ensure beings like this one are kept here for their talents to be wasted – she is very special.'

I went back to the little girl and told her: 'You're going to do amazing things in this world.'

At this point, more members of the girl's family came over to hear what was going on and her history was revealed to me. She'd been born with a weak heart and had had difficulties with it throughout her life, including three life-saving operations. I knew from what the angel was telling me that things had been touch-and-go and that angels had intervened many times to ensure that the little girl pulled through, particularly in the most recent instance.

The angel showed me that her most recent operation had gone wrong: she'd flatlined and been pronounced dead in theatre. The doctors had been pulling the white sheet over her when all of a sudden she'd taken a gasp of air and sat up, still connected to all of the monitors. Her recovery had been virtually instant and there was absolutely no medical explanation for it.

She told her family that she'd felt herself float out of her body and look down on the surgeons working on her. She could hear their conversations and also had a premonition of her mother's reaction to her passing. While she was watching this scene, a voice guided her back into her body and she was brought back to life.

When I related all this to the family, I could also confirm that the being recounting it to me was the angel who'd been responsible for bringing the little girl back to this plane. That angel was standing by her side now, ensuring that she was safe and bringing light to the family who adored her. It was a beautiful moment and I was so privileged to be part of it.

There are many examples of angels watching over children, but I don't often speak to children directly in the work I do, largely for practical reasons – they don't contact me at the newspaper or attend shows due to age restrictions, nor are they legally allowed to have readings until they are 18. The only places where I may be in touch with them are open seminars or events.

Recently, at such an event in Dundee, on the east coast of Scotland, a woman approached me with a small girl in a buggy. I could see a beautiful pink aura with hints of aqua all around it, indicating the child's energy. An angel was by the side of the buggy and when the woman said hello, I told her that she had a very sensitive child who was already surrounded by an angelic presence.

I could see the girl was very sensitive to changes in the environment and the energies around her, and said so.

The mother replied, 'Is that what's wrong with her? She seems a bit odd.'

I myself thought that was an odd thing to say. '"*Wrong*"?' I said. 'This is a gift your child has – she just isn't aware of how to control it.'

I added, 'I can see that things are hard at home.'

The mother then told me that her daughter had been diagnosed as autistic. I gently guided her to think that, irrespective of this diagnosis, she should approach her daughter's life with positivity and thank the angels for keeping her safe and protected from the lower energies that she herself was susceptible to. The woman admitted that she tended to get caught up in a negative mindset regarding her daughter, which I pointed out would not be doing the child any good at all, given her sensitivity.

I gave her daily affirmations from the angels to repeat and passed on information about how connected the girl was to her angels and how this would help her throughout her life.

I was once contacted by a family who wanted me to do private readings in their home, which was not too far from mine.

On arrival at the house, it was clear that the mother was very excited at having me there. Her angels came through very strongly and insisted that I spoke to her about her daughter. When I asked for more information, they told me that she was very gifted and intuitive – specifically, she'd seen the other side.

I told the woman all of this and she said, 'That's why I booked you. My 13-year-old daughter, Gemma, has been seeing spirits her whole life and we just don't know how to help her!'

The angels told me that Gemma was seeing everything – both positive and sometimes scary things. Although she wasn't scared herself, it was taking over her life and she found it hard to switch off, do her schoolwork or homework or even sleep.

We spoke about Gemma for some time and the angels insisted that I teach the young girl methods of protecting herself and switching off, so that she could still enjoy her life on this plane. I know more than anyone how hard it can be when there are interfering spirits turning up at every available opportunity, so I was happy to help.

We invited Gemma into the room. Her abilities were absolutely remarkable. She saw the spirit world absolutely everywhere and was very connected to it. However, she had never seen angels. I asked them why that was and they explained that although she was aware of spirits, she hadn't learned how to raise her vibration to that of angels yet.

I spoke to Gemma about her experiences and encouraged her to use my techniques for switching off and protecting her energy. I told her that her abilities would always be there if she felt the need to use them but she might find her calling in some other way, nothing was decided yet and she had to make her own choice, with guidance from the angels.

Some years passed and I learned that Gemma was studying to become a nurse. This was interesting to me as I know many psychics who were nurses before moving into my own type of work. It may very well be that Gemma has found a way to combine her interest in caring for others in more than one form. I'm sure I'll find out more as time goes on.

On one occasion I was doing a newspaper event and conducting onstage readings in Glasgow. It was a huge event and anyone could come along if they wanted to. Yvonne, the journalist from the *Scottish Sun* I mentioned earlier, was there and she wanted me to demonstrate angel communication for an article she was doing. She brought a lovely lady over to me who was holding hands with her four-year-old daughter. She told me her name was Isla and her little girl was called Kara.

Isla had a yellow aura – she was clearly fast-moving and always on the go. When there is too much yellow in an aura, it shows vitality issues. It's often seen in people with a vitamin deficiency. I asked the angels to give me some insight into Isla's life.

'Many changes have taken place recently,' they told me. 'Isla's home has been cleared of negative energy.'

When I said this, Isla gasped. 'Yes!' she cried.

In my mind, I saw her clearing out her whole home, giving it a complete going-over and even changing the doormat.

Isla said that was so true.

'It's wonderful that this has been done,' the angels went on, 'because her daughter was being affected by the old energy in the home. When Isla cleared it all out, it brought more light to her relationship with her partner. There is much love surrounding them, but lately there have been difficulties. There's now the chance of a fresh start, an opportunity for them all to move on.'

Isla looked very interested. 'True!' she said. 'It's all so true.'

'How has it affected Kara?' I asked the angels.

'She has had consistent ear blockages, which she herself created so that she didn't have to hear her parents argue.'

When I told Isla this, her eyes filled up with tears. 'This is true too. I can't believe you know she's had ear blockages. Now it makes sense why.'

The angels said: 'Don't worry, though, it's all changing from here – in a positive way. Please tell the girl we love her new bike!'

I bent down towards Kara and said, 'Hello! I've just been told you have a new bike – is that right?'

The shy little girl became excited, saying, 'It was my birthday yesterday and my daddy bought me a pink bike!'

I knew then that she was being looked after by angels.

As well as children, there's another group of innocent individuals who can communicate very effectively with angels – animals! Animals have angels too and their innocence and love make them perfect conduits for angelic communication with us as well.

Sometimes animals have elemental beings with them too, but not always. Elemental beings are from the angelic family but are more connected to the Earth. These are the beings people call 'fairies', the spiritual beings who surround nature, water, animals and all things connected to Mother Earth. I often see them around trees and animals and when I'm out connecting with nature. They are divinely created but can sometimes be fiery and hot-headed, just like us humans.

My awareness of this aspect of animal work developed when I visited a family friend. When I saw their dog, a golden Labrador called Lockie, I felt the animal's heart inside my own body. I knew he was suffering but that there were angels around him trying to bring healing. This situation emphasized to me that animals don't know how to ask for help. In that situation, I used my own powers of healing to help Lockie, to the amazement of his owner. This experience allowed me to consider the possibility of integrating animals' angels into my work, as well as the angels who help animals themselves.

This part of my work has been very important to me. On one occasion I was travelling to meet a local energy healer and palmist called Margaret. She lived in a beautiful house on the edge of town with ornate gates and a huge garden. As I was walking through the garden, I saw a small cat and beside it a big green angel. I said, 'Hello,' and asked why the angel was there in the garden with the cat.

The angel replied, 'This cat is in a state of distress. We're here to pass on the message to the owner.'

I knocked on the door and Margaret opened it.

'You're going to have to come outside,' I said. 'There's an angel out here with a distressed cat and it wants to pass on a message.' Not your usual sort of greeting, I have to admit!

I asked the angel what was wrong, expecting something quite traumatic, only to be told: 'The cat enjoys music. However, recently they've been playing it too loudly, especially with those new speakers. It just isn't fair, especially when he wants to sleep.'

Margaret told me, 'My husband, John, is deaf – he plays the guitar, but has had to get a special amplifier put in and it *is* really loud!'

Sometimes the messages I'm given from animals' angels are less superficial than that of the cat who wanted the music turned down! Some years ago, during a stage demonstration, I was drawn to a young woman called Ann. The angels wanted to bring through a young man from spirit who felt like her brother. Thomas told me that he'd passed over as the result of a terrible illness which had affected his blood. The angels informed me that he'd lived far from home and that it'd been very upsetting for his family, as they'd had difficulties getting to where he was based.

As the message progressed, Thomas kept emphasizing blood issues, which Ann confirmed were correct. Thomas passed on messages of love and support too and I felt that it was important to Ann to know that her brother was around her, giving her healing and love and saying she shouldn't feel guilty because she'd been unable to travel to where he'd lived when he was ill.

I saw a monkey sitting on Thomas' shoulder and told the audience this. They all laughed, but Ann was stunned. It transpires that Thomas had had HIV and had been living in Africa at the time. The monkey had been his pet.

Thomas' links with the creature also comforted Ann, as she knew that he'd been able to take reassurance from the bond he'd had with the animal at such a difficult time.

I'll never forget the time when I went to my best friend Teri's house. She was in the living room at the time, curling her mum's hair. I went in to join them for a chat and met her Auntie Nina, who was sitting on the couch. At her feet lay a lovely West Highland terrier called Max, who brought back so many fond memories of my dog, Tora. When I sat beside her, the small dog moved over and lay at my feet.

The angels said, 'Please give this dog some healing,' so I began to smooth his fur gently and then just placed my hands on him as he lay still, receiving the loving vibes I was sending him.

We were all chatting away, as Auntie Nina had a real interest in what I did, but she told me that she'd always found it hard to believe in spiritual things, as much as she loved the thought of it all, as she'd lost her son many years before.

Suddenly, she stopped talking and said, 'What are you up to with that dog?'

'I'm giving him some healing,' I replied. 'He seems in some sort of discomfort.'

'What do you mean, "discomfort"?' she asked, sounding worried.

The angels then stepped in and told me: 'This young dog has had issues with his teeth that have not been attended to.'

When I passed this on to Nina, she was absolutely stunned, as Max did have issues with his teeth. He was actually her daughter's dog and they'd been putting off taking him to the vet due to the cost.

I believe that the angels had ensured Max and I were put together that night so that he could receive love and healing to help his situation, and I felt so blessed to be a part of it.

One time my friend Clara and I were doing a psychic party in a great big fancy home in Renfrewshire, on the outskirts of Glasgow. I'd finished doing my four readings for the evening, but Clara was still in with her last client, Lesley. It had taken a while and she admitted she was struggling to make a connection to Lesley's family in heaven. (It happens!) She asked if I could go in to see if I could connect.

I asked the angels to intervene in the situation. Straightaway, they said: 'Her mother is here to speak.'

The energy of the mother came in immediately and I told Lesley about her condition and her peaceful passing in her sleep. She said it was all impressive and accurate.

'Angels,' I said, 'is there anything else we can tell this woman to prove that life exists after this one?'

Instantly I saw budgerigars flying around absolutely everywhere. They were buzzing across the room extremely fast!

When I told Lesley, she was amazed. Her family had run a budgie farm for years!

My own cat, Ralph, was named after Raphael, the healing archangel. I picked him up last Halloween and was so excited to be bringing him home. He was the last cat in his Ragdoll/Siamese litter and ended up being more Siamese than the rest, with wonderful bright blue eyes and a blue haze to his fur which glistened in the sunlight. I just felt the poor little guy needed a home, but I noticed one of his eyes was sore. The breeder assured me everything was fine, but said I could take some eye drops with me.

Ralph quickly found a favourite hiding place – a trouser rack in my wardrobe. He loved to sleep there in the heat and comfort, out of everyone's way.

On one of his first days at home, I had to leave him on his own while I was working. I generally only leave the house for five hours at a time, so I wasn't away for too long, but when I returned home, there he was in the trouser rack and neither of his eyes would open. All I could see were two slits.

It terrified the life out of me. I panicked and began to scream with worry. 'The angels can help me,' I told myself firmly.

I began by thanking Archangel Ariel ('Lioness of God') for helping Ralph and me with this situation (remember, don't ask for help, *thank* the angels for it to take fear out of the situation).

I was directed to use a wet cotton bud on Ralph's eyes. Once I rubbed it on them, his beautiful tiny blue eyes opened, but they were red and looked terribly sore. The poor little thing! I called in his namesake, Archangel Raphael, to bring healing and light to him. I had named him after the healing angel unconsciously, but I now believe it was because somehow I knew he would need healing at an early stage.

The next morning I took Ralph to the vet. They told me that he had cat flu, which he would have caught from his breeder's home. After he was treated, all was well – although I must say he's no angel now!

Just this year, my old schoolfriend Sean posted on Facebook that one of his kittens had run away. He'd been cat-sitting while his mum was on holiday and one of the little ones had disappeared. By the time I saw the message, it had been four days and Sean was beginning to get worried. He posted a picture of the cat on Facebook, asking if anyone could help.

My heart went out to Sean because I could just imagine how distressing the situation would be. I told him to say, 'Thank you, angels and Archangel Ariel, for directing my cat home.'

The next afternoon I received the following message:

> *I took your advice and ... my kitten came home this morning! I was hesitant about asking, but I did it and it apparently worked! Thank you!*

If I could get one message over to people it would be this: *Stop questioning; start believing.* What have you got to lose?

What You Can Do to Help

You can work with angels to help both children and animals. If you're having a difficult time with a child's behaviour or sensitivity, character or health, you can call on their angel to help with the situation quite easily. All you have to say is: 'Thank you, angel of [child's name], for helping bring light and love to this situation, all for the highest good.'

The other amazing thing you can do is teach your child to ask their angels for help. Tell your child that their angels are always with them and if they ever need help with anything at school or when walking home, or with their homework, or even when they cut their knee, their angels can help. All they have to say is: 'Thank you, angels, for helping me!' When they do this, their sensitivity will draw their angels near to them and they'll be wrapped up in golden angelic energy to help heal their situation.

A great thing you can do too is to ask them to draw their guardian angel. Get a large selection of coloured pencils and some paper and say: 'What do you think your angel looks like?' Ask them the colour of the angel's clothes and skin, whether they're large or small, short or tall, what their hair is like, whether they have wings or shoes, whether they are holding anything or have someone with them. Once you've fired their imagination, encourage them to draw their angel. You'll be pleasantly surprised by the wisdom your little one will produce and it will strengthen their connection with their angel too.

As already mentioned, I generally pray to angels as a force rather than call on one angel specifically, because that way the right angel will be delivered to do the job. However, Archangel Ariel has a remarkable connection with animals and can help with everything to do with them – anything from finding a lost pet to finding your pet a new home. If you specifically want help with healing an animal, it's also great to bring in Archangel Raphael to join Ariel.

You can assist angels in healing your pet by laying your hands on the animal for comfort. One hand behind the crown and one on the heart area always works. Once you feel ready to change position, put one hand in the middle of the animal's back and one at the bottom of their spine to ground them.

When you lay your hands on the animal, you can say: 'Thank you, angels, for allowing me to channel your healing light to [animal's name], all for the highest good.'

As the healing begins, watch the animal relax into the healing rays. If it randomly gets up and walks away, it's because it's had enough healing for that day. Animals are intelligent and can often see healing energy; they'll know when they've had enough.

Chapter 9

SO TINY, SO IMPORTANT

So many of the people who book readings with me or come to my shows begin by saying that they're sceptical or don't believe any of this 'stuff'. But very often they're the ones who receive particularly strong messages.

One winter evening a lady called Georgina came to my office for a reading. Immediately she said that she was sceptical, but angels appeared for her very quickly. I started, as always, by giving her a personality and present feelings reading, then invited her angels to come closer. They brought with them a lady from spirit and said that she was Georgina's grandmother.

This woman was beautiful, with an amazing aura, and I was aware that she was honest with a fiery heart. She was so excited at being able to speak to her granddaughter and wanted to pass on advice and love, but I was aware that Georgina's scepticism could result in the message being unheeded. Despite the fact that I'd been accurate with everything I'd told her about herself, she'd continued to protest that she didn't really 'believe'.

Now I told her her grandmother's name, the illness she'd died from and her memories of her passing in hospital, but she still seemed unconvinced.

I had to request more evidence. Finally, Georgina's grandmother showed me a jar of face cream. I had to smile, because so often it really is the dullest, most trivial little things that made people believe. I told Georgina about the face cream – and she opened her handbag and brought out the same pot.

'This is my grandmother's cream,' she told me. 'It was all I kept of her and I carry it everywhere.'

Convinced by this remarkable detail, Georgina opened herself to angelic communication and I helped her and her grandmother re-establish their loving bond.

These tiny details are sometimes the only things that convince people of the existence of angels. There have been so many examples over the years.

A lady called Lee initially contacted me by email. I remember she said that she didn't want to incur any financial outlay if she wasn't going to receive useful guidance or evidence from her angels or loved ones in spirit! I reassured her about my 'no evidence, no fee' policy and she arrived for a reading on a cold winter's day with icy roads and freezing temperatures.

I asked her to say a short internal prayer for her family and angels to come through while she placed her hands on the angel cards and immediately I saw an angel beside her. This angel told me that her life had been a real roller coaster. I was shown tough times in her childhood and with her relationships. The angel went on to tell that the year we were in would be both the best and the worst of her life: 'She will know what it is like to be settled and she will know what it is like to have her heart broken.'

The angel went on to tell me that the angels were ready to bring in the spirits of Lee's loved ones and I asked them to step forwards.

'Tell her that Margaret is here,' the angel said. 'She passed away in her own home and it was very quick. Tell Lee that she thought a lot of her.'

Margaret was joined by a young man named Robert. By this point, Lee was extremely emotional. Robert wanted to apologize for his 'silly moves', which was an extreme euphemism for what he showed me – he'd actually overdosed on heroin.

It transpired that Robert had been Lee's partner and Margaret had been his mother – they had passed within three months of each other. The angels who were beside them wanted to offer their support to Lee and make me aware of ongoing arguments she'd had with a family member since their passing. There had been an issue about payment for the funerals. Lee took this specific detail as remarkable confirmation of the connection I had.

The angels went on to tell me of Lee's three children. One in particular, a girl, was very spiritual and there were many angels around her. The angels' guidance for Lee was to move on, knowing that Robert was by her side, but also to ensure that she didn't spend the rest of her life alone. Lee told me that this was what her ex-partner had always told her. Much emotion was released during the session and I conducted some spiritual healing.

Lee's story reminds me of that of another sceptical woman I worked with when I was only 16 and at the start of my journey. This woman's scepticism wasn't about spiritual connections in general, though, just about me in particular!

At a training session at the airport one day, the other participants found out about my talent and were intrigued – all but one girl, Louise, who was very defensive. She told me that her brother-in-law was a renowned medium and that she was an expert in the subject herself.

As the day progressed, everyone was keen for me to show my talent, so I agreed to do some readings when we finished and I said that I'd speak to their guardian angels. I made my way round them all, giving them individual details and making predictions. By the time I made it to Louise, she was clearly interested but still reserved.

There was a light blue angel at her side who told me that she was a mother and had a lovely feisty daughter who would do very well with Louise's encouragement. The angel also showed me the spirit of another girl, one who had passed over, saying that Louise shouldn't blame herself for the loss of this child.

Louise burst into tears and said that she'd never expected anything so accurate and relevant to come up in just a quick reading. She actually became a close supporter of my work and encourages me to this day.

Louise wasn't the only sceptic to be amazed by the power of angels. Once I travelled to a house in Uddingston, south of Glasgow, to read for a few ladies. On arrival, I explained how I worked, but there was a man in the room, the husband of one of the women, who was very arrogant and dismissive of me.

I told him, as I always do, that I don't have a problem with sceptics as long as they accept it when I do prove the existence of angels to them, but he still talked over me and made nasty comments as I tried to explain my work to the women. When I pointed out that this was difficult for them all, he said, 'If you're so psychic, read my mind then. I'll think of something and you just tell me what it is. That shouldn't be hard, should it? Not for someone as talented as you.'

I replied that I didn't want to stoop to that level and that I wasn't actually a mind reader, but the man continued to heckle me. Things were becoming difficult.

I mentally asked the angels to help and one replied, 'His shoulder has been frozen for weeks – tell him that.'

As soon as I repeated those words, the man's face fell and he jumped out of his seat, muttering that he was going to take the dog for a walk!

When he left, his wife revealed that he had indeed got a bad shoulder that had refused to get better despite lots of different therapies. He never did return that night!

A favourite story of mine concerns the time a lovely lady called Bernadette came to my home for a reading. She was really warm and generous and was desperate to hear anything I could pass on to her.

The angels told me that she was in a caring profession, loved what she did and was a real beacon of light for her clients. They brought forward her mother, Katie. She was incredibly like Bernadette, both in features and personality. As she began communicating with my angels, I could see that in the past Bernadette had been running around dealing with her work but caring for her mother too.

It had been a real struggle for Bernadette, but she'd just got on with it because it was what she thought was best. As the reading progressed, the angels began surrounding her in loving pink healing energy to help remove the weight from her heart and shoulders. They told me that since her mother's passing, she hadn't let much emotion out and everything had been building up.

Katie wanted to thank her daughter for making sure she never went into a home and ensuring she stayed in her family's care. Out of nowhere, I suddenly saw a pair of hands spilling cocktail sticks onto a table. When I passed this on, Bernadette couldn't believe it. In the week of her passing, her mother had bought a huge crate of cocktail sticks for no reason, and to this day Bernadette kept it in her wardrobe because it reminded her of her mum. This was the trivial yet special evidence that showed her that her amazing mother was well in heaven.

A young bank worker named Charlie once contacted me for a reading. He wanted to get in touch with his brother-in law, Harry, who had passed very suddenly after a tragic car crash that had left many unanswered questions for his family.

I'd known Harry myself and asked Charlie to bring some items of significance in a bag for me to use as an aid to contact heaven. I didn't use these in the end to make a connection, but I found this reading particularly difficult because I didn't want to say anything that Charlie could dismiss as coming from my prior knowledge of Harry rather than from angels. I knew I was giving myself a hard time here. I also knew Harry was OK, but I had to prove it to Charlie, and in a way that he could believe.

When I called my angels into my mind and asked them to tell me one thing I could give as evidence to Charlie, I saw a wheel in my head. I said: 'I have to tell you about the wheel.'

Charlie didn't understand. Actually, he was a bit angry. Yes, his brother-in-law had died in a car and they'd both loved cars, but why would he tell him about a wheel?

We moved on to speak about other things through the angels, especially Charlie's idea of starting up as self-employed while retaining his other job. This was all accurate information and he seemed happy, but I still wasn't really satisfied and as we neared the end of the reading I asked him if he'd brought any items he wanted me to work with.

Opening his bag, Charlie revealed a wheel-shaped clock. Excited, I said, 'The wheel! That's your evidence that Harry is with you!'

Charlie began to laugh. 'I can't believe that's what it was,' he said. 'I never even thought about it.'

It turned out that his brother-in-law had bought the wheel clock for Charlie's son for Christmas and it was a cherished family item now because Harry had passed not long afterwards.

Angels and spirits amaze me more and more every day!

Chapter 10

SIGNS FROM ABOVE

Angels love to send us a reminder of their presence. They'll use anything they can to highlight their presence in our heart and mind. Symbols and signs come in all shapes and sizes. When you see a sign, it can really heighten your faith in angels, or even convert you into a complete believer. When I see signs that angels are indeed real and are communicating through these reminders, it absolutely rocks my world.

The best-known sign that angels are present is a little white feather somewhere unusual, somewhere there's no chance it could have got to any other way, but they send a lot of other signs too. You'll know it's a sign when something pops up and there's no possible human explanation for it or the synchronicity is just too amazing. Many people write to me about their angel experiences and signs, and I have to admit some of them are incredible – to the point that they make every hair on my body stand on end. But the real question is: how do signs work? And why do angels send them to us?

In the last five years I've met more angel believers than ever and a lot of them have come to rely on signs to prove that angels are real, but I have to be honest and say this isn't the true point of them.

I've found that angels love to send us signs almost as a smile. They seem to show up more clearly than ever when we trust these divine beings and when we're on the right path.

Someone recently asked me, 'How do I know what the sign means?'

I asked them to elaborate.

'Well,' they said, 'I've asked the angels to give me a sign to tell me whether this is the right choice or not!'

Then it all made sense.

Angels will send you a sign when you're on the right path. But if you're relying on signs to tell you what's right and what's wrong then you're going to start getting confused, and so are your angels.

When a sign appears in your life, know your angels are smiling down upon you and whispering, 'Good work, friend,' because really that's what they're doing.

To clarify: signs arrive when you're on the right path to remind you there's an ever-present love with you, guiding you. Even though you may feel challenged, alone or emotional at times, know that miracles are occurring to help you on.

Visits from Heaven

Not only do angels send us signs, but our loved ones in the spirit world do too. If they know a way of sending you a message, they absolutely will.

A while back I conducted a private session for a gentleman. Let's call him Steve. Nothing came through, but after leaving it for 12 months we both decided to try again. This time we connected with his dad, Andrew, in spirit. He was a true gentleman and really wanted to show his loving support for his son. I was able to give his name, how he'd passed away and what his personality was like, but I still felt that there needed to be an 'Aha!' moment for Steve.

I remember closing my eyes and just giving a silent call to Steve's dad, saying, 'I'm so grateful that you're here today. Thank you for giving more evidence of your presence so I can confirm to your son that you're really here with us!'

As I opened my eyes I clairvoyantly saw a magpie fly by Steve. I felt my right arm come up and I saluted, saying out loud, 'Good afternoon, Mr Magpie.'

Steve couldn't control his tears – this confirmed that his dad was with us from heaven. It turned out that he'd regularly said hello to magpies. Morning, noon and night, it was a daily ritual for him.

Since his father's passing, Steve had seen magpies literally everywhere he went. Not only that – every morning there'd be a single magpie in his garden and it reminded him of his dad so much. It could only be a coincidence, he thought, but he often asked himself, 'Is this a sign?' or even 'Is it Dad?' Now he had spiritual confirmation of what he had intuitively felt.

Have You Seen a Sign?

Has something synchronistic happened to you that you can't explain? Do you regularly see something in your daily life that reminds you of your angels or loved ones in heaven? Do you see something that makes you think that you're not alone and that you're loved or that there's a message there for you?

If so, it's important that you stop thinking you're imagining things or wondering how it possibly could have happened and start accepting that a miracle has taken place. I try not to, but sometimes I get really frustrated with people when they tell me they think they've seen a sign but they don't know. When something amazing happens, you need to recognize it and you need to say thank you.

I like to say to people it's like getting a postcard or a letter from a loved one in a faraway country. When you receive it, you want to say thank you or tell them in some way that you understand what they're saying, don't you? Well, it's exactly the same with signs from heaven. When you see a sign, acknowledge it. If you begin to question what's happened, you're lowering your vibe and breaking your connection to heaven, and it can take a lot of work and patience to get it back. When I see a sign, I immediately give thanks and, if I can, take some time to check in (using my tuning-in technique; *see pages 26-27*) to see if I can receive any guidance.

Different Types of Sign

When I spent time at Spiritualist church I learned so much about signs and the many different ways angels and spirits can send them. I learned that they can use all of our senses and more to direct their loving guidance our way. They'll use what's already around us and bring our attention to it using our natural sensitivity and intuition.

Electronics

Angels seem to have their own magical way with electronics and so does the spirit world (especially with lights and TVs). I've experienced my phone turning itself on and off, channels changing and other weird occurrences where my laptop sticks on an angel picture with a message and more. Heaven loves to use what we have around us and a lot of the time that's electronics, so when things don't work properly, don't be surprised. You're receiving a visit!

Manifestations

Angels will use things around us to get our attention, but I truly believe they have the ability to manifest things too. A common example is finding a feather in the strangest of places, where there's no way for it to have got there other than materializing from thin air. In the Spiritualist church circle I attended, I learned from one of the senior healers that in the past, when something arrived from nowhere in a séance, they called it an 'apport'.

Nature

Angels adore nature, so they can easily work with the laws of nature to send you a message. They can send a shape in a cloud, a vegetable shaped like a love heart, and God only knows what else. I remember my mum found the most perfect heart-shaped potato one night after she'd said some prayers in the kitchen while making dinner. She felt it was a sign that heaven was smiling upon her.

Numbers

This is one of my favourite ways that angels get in touch. I actually learned about it through the world's leading angel expert Doreen Virtue. She taught me that numbers lining up on a digital clock could be messages from heaven and the universe – and I've seen it happening ever since. Here's my interpretation of a couple of the configurations:

> 11:11 – You are the one with everything that is and ever will be right now. As you are connected to the oneness of the universe, the angels are encouraging you to think in a positive way about your life and world. Your thoughts and actions are creating and carving your path ahead, so focus on your dreams and aspirations with unwavering faith.
>
> 22:22 – You are influencing all those who surround you right now. If you're looking for a change, then you must be that change. How can you be kinder, more loving and supportive of those who surround you today? When you focus on peace, support and essentially how you can serve, you will be served.

Sounds and Music

Angels love music. In fact they're the most incredible singers. There's a category of angels called the Seraphim who are said to sing the praises of the creator constantly. I've woken up many times to the most beautiful sounds and songs that have no other explanation than an angelic one.

Because angels love music so much, they allow it to be their messenger. They'll encourage us to turn on the radio at specific times, change the channel or walk into a store when specific songs are playing, so we can get a message from the lyrics.

Symbols

The angels love little symbols and they love using them to tell us they're present. They can make us notice things in our daily life that look like wings, feathers or even the outline of an angel.

Winged Creatures

Angels themselves have been seen as winged creatures and they work closely with the animal and insect realm to send us messages. Everything from bees to birds can bring us messages from the angels and the spirit world.

Words

Angels love using words to direct us to them too. Have you ever noticed a word you just needed to hear while driving along the road? Have you ever seen a van pulling in front of you with the message you needed right at that moment? Well, heaven has sent those messages too.

Understanding Signs

I recently joined my dear friend Gabby Bernstein on stage in London to speak about the power of signs. One audience member asked us how she could understand them, because although she recognized them, she never really knew what they meant. One thing that came to me during our conversation that day was the fact that so often we try and work signs out ourselves rather than going straight to the source and asking the angels to reveal the message to us. So while I was standing there in front of, say, 350 people, this prayer dropped into my mind and just poured from my heart:

> *'Thank you, angels, for revealing within me ways I can understand your signs and know you are here!'*

I remember we said the prayer together and I vowed to myself that this would become a regular part of my spiritual practice.

When it comes to spirit and the angels, some things just can't be Googled – you've got to go within. Then, through meditation, you'll understand your message. The first thing I do when I see a sign is say thanks, but I 'feel' into it afterwards.

To start you off, I've put together a bunch of my favourite signs from heaven and the messages I believe they represent. There are so many signs that I'd probably need a whole book to tell you about them all, but what's really important is that the angels will develop their own language with you – they'll figure out what will speak to you and then work with that. So if you see something regularly and don't know what it means, you need to do the work and find out yourself. If you ask the angels, they'll be glad to help you.

Note that these signs don't have to be the actual thing – you could see them on stuffed toys, letters, emails and who knows what else.

Bees

As bees work together in a community to create their honey, they remind us to work together in a team to create positive and sweet changes in the world. Also, because bees are so important to the preservation of the Earth, when we see them, angels are thanking us for all the hard work we're doing for others, because it's making the world a better place.

Butterflies

The butterfly has long been known as a symbol of transformation. I've found that butterflies arrive on our path when we're going through great change and overcoming previous challenges. However, I've also found they come to us when we've lost a loved one who went through pain – they let us know they've overcome the diseases of the Earth and are now free.

Coins

I've always believed that coins represent loved ones in heaven, in particular grandparents. It's as though they're coming through and offering us a little shiny penny to give us a push in the right direction and wish us luck.

Dolphins

Dolphins are some of the angels' most treasured beings on Earth. They are the angels of the sea. They represent family, freedom and deep bonds of friendship and trust. When we continually see dolphins, angels are encouraging us to have fun, be free and enjoy the friends and family we have around us.

Dragonflies

Dragonfly energy represents going on a journey. When dragonflies keep appearing on our path, angels want us to know that they're with us the whole way. There are loads of blessings surrounding the dragonfly, because it shows we're making huge progress on our journey.

Feathers

Feathers are the best-known angel sign. Angels absolutely love sending them to us. Finding a feather is like being given an angelic business card or love note. The feathers can be any colour, but sometimes the colour has a message of its own:

Dark Feathers: The angels are absorbing your pain or any other challenging emotions you're dealing with at this time. Take some time to ask for the extra support you need and deserve from heaven.

White Feathers: Your guardian angel wants you to know they're close by and they know about your prayers and/or current situation. They're asking you to remain positive.

Ladybirds/Ladybugs

These little red insects are a symbol of happiness and peace. Ever since I was a child I've instinctively known that they're lucky little beings. When they appear in our life, angels want us to know they're present and are smoothing the road ahead for us.

Magpies

These lovely birds have had different meanings over the years. I truly believe they show up to say a loved one is sending their love and watching over us. If we see a cluster of magpies, each one represents a loved one in heaven looking down on us.

Money

When we continually find money in random places, on our path, or even in clothing we've not worn in a while, angels are sending us financial support and security. We're being asked to open up all channels to receive the abundance we truly deserve.

Music

Music brings people together; it brings joy and encourages us to dance. When we hear a song over and over again, we're being asked to pay careful attention to the lyrics or even the song name – there's a message for us within.

Rainbows

When we see rainbows all around us, it's a promise from the universe that our prayers will soon be answered. Rainbows encourage us to have faith because the angels have faith in us.

Robins

Robins bring a message from a loved one, especially during a deep period of grief or if someone has recently passed.

The message is: 'I am here with you now!' As robins are territorial little birds, there's a chance they'll visit regularly and make our territory theirs, so they can become the perfect messengers for a close loved one.

Stars

Seeing stars everywhere we go is a message from heaven thanking us for a job well done. Angels want us to know that they are so proud of us and that they're aware of our achievements and the transformations we've made.

Be Open to Signs

I've found that asking for signs is cool, but it's creating openness within that encourages them to manifest. Sure you can ask the angels to send you a specific sign, but sometimes that means you'll be waiting longer than you'd like. I prefer to hand myself over completely to the angels and by the grace of God they'll send something my way that assures me they're close by.

In all honesty, when my journey into this world began, I'd always ask for a sign to know the angels were close, but as I trusted in them more, I asked less. I discovered very quickly that when you're on this path and in constant communication with angels through a daily spiritual practice, you'll be blessed by signs and blown away by how strong they grow to be.

If you want to ask the angels to give you a sign, try the following:

Visualize yourself surrounded by golden light. See it moving right over you. This makes your connection to the angels even stronger. It's like broadband for your prayers.

If you find it challenging to visualize, you can say the affirmation: 'I am immersed in golden light. It has washed over my body from head to toe.'

Now say, with loving intentions, 'Thank you, angels, for reminding me of your presence!'

You can add on some gratitude, if you like. This really enhances the angelic connection. I often say: 'It feels so good to know you're here. I'm so thankful we're on this journey together!'

Now let go and let God! Let the angels bless you with their presence.

Chapter 11

HELP FROM ABOVE

If angels are determined to help us, then they will. Even if they can't change a situation, they'll support us through it.

One example of this really stands out in my mind. When I was about 15, my mum was struggling with her finances. We're very close and I knew that she was constantly worried about the difficult time we were having with money. I kept reminding her that angels were there to help her and could do plenty if she'd just ask. But although my mum had been fully aware for years that her one and only child was spending the best part of every day chatting away with angels, she wasn't about to start randomly doing so herself. She's a very practical woman and though she's always supported me in every way imaginable, in those early years she did roll her eyes a fair bit when I told her to just ask the angels! She should have known by then – she certainly knows by now – that it was the right thing to do, but there was a part of her just not committing to the idea.

I may have been psychic and I may have been communicating with angels, but I was also an annoying never-give-up teenager when I had to be. So my mum got the full force of it.

'*Why* won't you do it, Mum? *Why* won't you ask the angels to help?'

Looking back, I probably did go on a bit, but I was convinced, due to everything I'd already witnessed, that this was the right thing to do. Then, as now, I can't quite understand *why* people won't access something which is sitting there waiting for them and which will make their life so much easier.

I don't know whether my mum just got fed up of me or whether I did manage to convince her with my fantastic persuasive skills (which consisted mostly of saying over and over again, 'Go on, Mum, go on! Just talk to them, Mum! Ask them to help you, Mum!'), but finally she caved in.

'Right then, Kyle,' she said one day, 'what do I do? How do I get angels to get this sorted for me, because no one else is?'

I told her that she had to ask the angels of abundance to come in and assist her that month. She needed to tell them that she wanted help to pay her bills and get through until her wages came in. She nodded as I spoke, but didn't do or say anything in front of me. I left it after that. I'd done as much as I could, but I also sensed that I'd gone far enough – Mum had to take the next step.

The next day, a Monday, I got a call on my mobile. My mum was shrieking down the line at me.

'It's happened, Kyle! It's happened!'

'What has? What's happened?' I asked, totally confused.

'Well, I did what you said and asked the angels of abundance for help.'

I kept quiet. The fact that Mum had actually done that was amazing enough. I was pretty sure she'd have got some help by communicating with them, so it was the fact that she'd done it in the first place that was the miracle to me.

'I've just had some money through from a credit card company,' Mum went on. 'They owed me £250 in overcharging and I had absolutely no idea about it. I never contacted them about the money, I didn't even know they owed it me, but here it is, in my account.'

I knew it was the work of angels. This random sum was enough for Mum to pay her bills until her wages came in and get her through that difficult month.

For me, that was evidence of the power of angels and the ways in which they are obliged to help us. Now if Mum had asked for lottery numbers, she wouldn't have been sent them. If it's a request based on greed, it won't happen, but Mum only needed a bit of cash to get her through and she wasn't harming anyone else with her request, so the angels judged that this was worthwhile. There's always help waiting for us, if only we ask.

I'm often asked why angels want to help us at all. I suppose that's a valid enough question really. Quite simply, they want to help us because it's their *purpose*. It's what they exist for. They see our happiness as their sole aim. The universal life-force that oversees all we do has created angels to guide, guard and protect us. These amazing beings might be seen to have a bit of a hard time of it, lumped with us all day, every day, but they do it willingly. They want to help us reach our highest potential and obtain the most from all of our learning experiences in this life.

And do you know what? We're not always as bad as we think ... and angels can help us to recognize that and be a bit easier on ourselves.

One of the best lessons I received was when I worked with a lady called Angela. She was sceptical of everything and found it hard to believe that anyone – angel or not – would want to do anything good for her. I've seen this so many times, and it's a terrible thing to see people cover themselves with armour, thinking that it will give them protection when it's really just putting up a barrier between themselves and the rest of the world. So the way in which Angela was presenting herself to the world was causing her problems. They were of her own making, but she simply couldn't see it.

After explaining how everything worked, I asked her to lay her hands on top of my angel cards as I tuned in. Her guardian angel was very close by and I couldn't help feeling that she'd often communicated with that angel. She was sceptical about psychics, but definitely not about angels and the afterlife. The angel then told me her father was there to speak to her.

I instantly saw an image of Angela as a child and her father walking out on the family. I then saw an image of her in her twenties and her father trying to speak to her, but she wasn't interested; she simply turned her back.

When I told her what was being shown to me, she tried to hold back her tears. Then the name 'Bill' came into my head.

'That's my dad's name,' she said and began to weep. 'He walked out on us because he and my mum just didn't see eye to eye. He tried to speak to me on my 21st birthday and I just wasn't interested. It took his passing away before I forgave him for leaving us.'

Then I could see an image of Angela standing at the front door of a home and a lovely elderly lady handing her what seemed to be photographs.

When I asked what this was, she said, 'I went to meet my dad's new wife and she gave me photographs of him. She was a lovely woman and it helped my heart to heal seeing these images.'

It turned out that Angela had waited years for a psychic to bring her father through and to know he was happy where he was and, ultimately, that she was loved.

As her father moved back to the light, I heard, 'Raphael is real!'

Angela was shocked. From under her T-shirt she pulled out a pendant that contained the symbol and name of Archangel Raphael. This showed that all was well.

During the reading I also heard some interesting facts such as: 'stroke' and 'I'. It turned out that Angela's stepfather had had a stroke and was currently on a ventilator.

Her guardian angel stepped forwards and spoke in very plain English saying, 'As much as you like to be hands on with the homeless, we angels are ensuring you help with the bigger picture. You might not feel 100 per cent sure about the office you've been moved to, but you are there for a reason, and an opportunity will arise where you can help more people than you ever have before.'

Angela worked for a homeless shelter and had recently been moved to an office where she felt helpless because she wasn't working with families directly. However, she accepted that it was for reasons she just couldn't see yet.

This reading really proved angels want to assist our paths in life so that we live to our highest potential and get the most out of all of our learning experiences.

The help angels give often amazes even me. When I was doing a reading for a young woman called Sarah, the scene became emotional very quickly. I was aware of angels all around immediately. There was a great deal of uncertainty concerning self-confidence and love, and I felt the need for Sarah to forgive herself. The angels showed me her aura, which was green. A green aura signifies approachability. It comes from the heart and indicates caring. It shows that person practises altruism without thinking twice about it – they are a giving soul who has time and patience for people. So Sarah was a caring person, but there was a great deal of grief inside her heart. The angels said that she'd never been settled since the loss of a child: 'She has been unfaithful to her husband ever since she lost her daughter to spirit. She is looking for happiness, but she won't find it that way. Healing must come from within. Until she knows that her child is safe in spirit, she will never settle.'

At this point, the angels brought the energy of a child into the room and said, 'Millie's here!'

Sarah became very emotional and said, 'That's her, that's what my baby was called!'

I was also hit by the impact of this and started to cry. Reuniting a mother with her child so that she could truly move on, knowing that her baby was safe in spirit, was a powerful experience.

Sarah's angels wanted to heal her heart, but she needed to know that her daughter's passing wasn't her fault and that she shouldn't be replacing the pain of the loss with the guilt that comes from being unfaithful. Her angels guided her to embrace the support of her loving husband instead of pushing him away, and she admitted she loved him deeply but had never known what to do with her grief.

Thanks to the angels, Sarah learned that she could move on with her daughter by her side and in her heart.

Ally was a woman who hosted an evening of readings for friends and was the last of the group to sit with me. I felt that this would be very different from all the other readings I'd done that night and told her to respond only by saying 'yes' or 'no'.

The angels told me that Ally was a very energetic, lively type of person with the great ability to be perfectly honest in all situations. She was a simple person in that she didn't place much value in material things. There was an amazing blue angel standing by her side who told me that it was the Angel of Truth. When I told Ally this, she looked rather sceptical, but when I went on to say that the angel was there because her son needed support and encouragement, she was much more convinced.

As I tried to read more of Ally's life, the information became jumbled and there were pieces of information all over the place. Patiently Ally waited as I communicated with my own angels as well as hers and tried to figure out what was going on. She interrupted to say that she wasn't really there for herself but would like to hear more about her son. She wanted to know what was next for him.

When I asked the angels about this, they put me in a courtroom and I could see myself being wrongly accused. Angels often use me as a surrogate in an experience so that I can get an idea of what is going on. I felt as if there was an issue relating to Ally's son's life both professionally and in relation to him being emotionally connected with an immature female character. It turned out that he'd been accused of sexually assaulting a work colleague when the fact was that they'd just drunkenly got together.

The Angel of Truth stepped back in with a woman from spirit named Rosie. They wanted to assure Ally that her son hadn't done what he was accused of and that justice would prevail. Everything became much clearer and Ally was finally relieved by what she was told.

Some weeks passed before I had an email from her to say that everything had turned out well and her family was now moving fearlessly in the right direction.

Recently I did a reading for a woman named Eileen who was a bright and bubbly character. She was a curvaceous woman with glasses and long, naturally curly blonde hair.

Her angels told me that I was to pass on information about how her life had always been lived for others. She had spent her time in service to other people, ensuring that everyone was looked after. I said, 'You're a "yes" person, aren't you?' When she responded, 'Yes,' we both laughed!

I saw loving pink angels coming into the room to join us and I could also see two male spirits with Eileen. I was told that one of them was her father and the other was a child who had gone to heaven and had now grown up into a young man. They were both called Robert.

When I asked the angels why they'd brought Eileen to me, they told me they wanted to help her with her fears and guilt about being a mother. It turned out that young Robert had gone to heaven when Eileen had had a termination.

The angels said: 'The universe and this child aren't blaming Eileen, she's blaming herself. We know this has caused many issues in her life, including issues with her reproductive system. At the time she didn't feel ready to be a mother, but this fear and guilt then stopped her from having a child later in life.'

With her eyes filling with tears, Eileen said that made so much sense. She hadn't been in a position to be a mother when she'd been pregnant with Robert and when she'd finally met a partner to settle down with, she'd experienced menopause at the age of just 29, which had stopped her from having another baby.

The angels acknowledged the ability to love and care for others that Eileen put out every day in her work and in looking after her elderly mother. Even though she'd always hoped to be a mother herself, Eileen was now able to forgive herself and move on, knowing the spirit of her baby was fine and well. She'd always felt she'd taken him from the world, but now she knew he was just in another world, growing, developing and guiding her as he would have done had he been here.

It was such an emotional reading and it brought so much healing. Eileen's father, Robert, then came through strong and to the point. He was looking at his watch because I'd been running late for the reading!

'He was a right joker, your dad, wasn't he?' I laughed and Eileen confirmed this was true.

Her father wanted Eileen to pass on to her mother that he was still with her and that she had to slow down. When I asked why this message was important, I was told she had angina and often got herself in a panic. If she could just slow her routine down slightly, she'd get less bothered by everything.

Eileen gladly passed on the information to her mum, who was overjoyed to have advice from her husband – the one person she would listen to. A huge part of her life was just spent keeping busy to keep her mind off loneliness. Knowing her late husband was still with her was a relief.

The link between parents and children is, naturally, often one of the strongest, but I've conducted many readings in which that link has been difficult, to say the least. In fact I've worked with a lot of abuse cases over the years. One which stuck out in particular was that of a woman named Shirley.

When Shirley sat down for her reading, I knew she was going to make my work hard for me because she wasn't giving anything away. She had a strong red aura which showed that she never liked to reveal too much. She'd learned to be like that in order to defend herself.

When I asked the angels why this defence mechanism had been created, they told me it was due to the abusive relationship she'd had with her father. I knew I'd been thrown right into the deep end here, but I had to go straight to the issue. It took her by surprise and she quietly said, 'I thought you'd at least ease me in gently.'

The angels told me that her father was with us and wanted to apologize for abusing his daughter here on Earth.

'I've worked on this,' Shirley said, 'with counsellors and other professionals, but I've always felt I couldn't move on until I heard it from him.'

As we continued with the reading, Shirley's mother's energy came into the room from heaven. The angels told me that she wanted to apologize for not supporting or believing Shirley. She just hadn't been able to face the subject at all, with the result that it had all just been suppressed.

'That is so true,' said Shirley, sadly.

The angels went on to say that this pattern had followed Shirley throughout her life and she'd never experienced a settled and loving relationship as a result, despite desperately wanting this to happen.

'That's true too,' she admitted.

The angels showed me Shirley in a relationship with someone, but when I looked at the man in my mind, I felt he wasn't in the right place. He had a ring on his finger and I knew he wasn't married to Shirley – she was having a relationship with a married man. When I gave her this information, she again nodded.

'She's scared of commitment from others, so she has attracted someone into her life who can't commit,' the angels said.

It all made sense.

Shirley's father came in with the angels when we cut the cords. As we did this, the name 'Danny' came into my head.

'That was my dad's name!' Shirley said. 'Now I know he's really here!'

Once we cut the cords, Shirley forgave her parents and herself. The angels guided her to work on some self-love affirmations and prayers which she could use help start her life afresh. It was a beautiful ending to a sad story.

One of the most touching readings I've ever done was for a woman in her fifties called Marie.

When she first walked into the room, all of the spirits and angels around her were extremely keen to start the reading. They told me that she lived near to a hospital and showed me the Govan area of Glasgow – a rough, working-class area. They then informed me that she'd grown up there. As things progressed, they said that her husband was having a tough time connected to his work but that good things lay ahead. Again, they gave geographical details by showing where he commuted to each day.

I asked whether there was anyone in spirit who wanted to contact Marie, and the angels brought forwards her grandmother. I felt that she had had a great deal to do with Marie's upbringing and had taught her everything she knew. The angels then brought in Marie's birth mother and showed that there was a distance between them, as she hadn't always communicated openly with her daughter. Marie said that there was a lot that had never been spoken about between them.

At this point, the angels wished to bring in something I call 'parent healing' (*see page 144*) to help Marie with all of the hurt and negative emotions connected with her mother. They passed on her story to me, which was that her mum had been an unmarried girl of only 17 when she'd become pregnant in the 1950s. She'd been sent away to give birth, and when she'd returned, her own mother, the spirit I'd communicated with earlier, had taken over her maternal role. A lot of emotion was released in this session and Marie's mother was more communicative in spirit than she'd ever been on this plane.

At the end of the session, Marie remarked that she'd never really known for certain who her father was. When I asked the angels, they immediately replied, 'Samuel.'

When Marie was given this name, she was shocked. She pulled out an old photograph and said, 'That's Samuel. I always thought he was my father, but no one ever confirmed it. I carry this around because I always hoped that one day I'd find out for sure – and now you've given me that.'

Parent Healing

This is the process I use when someone has had issues with a parent. That parent could be on Earth or in heaven – it works either way. It is useful for when you want to forgive your parent and you want your parent to forgive you. You can use it to heal situations with anyone; however, I specifically use it for parental work.

In your mind, imagine yourself sitting across from your parent in a room on nice comfortable sofas.

In your mind, begin to speak **lovingly** *to your parent and forgive them for everything that has happened between you. If you're looking to be forgiven for something yourself, imagine your parent forgiving you for your actions.*

Once you've got everything off your chest, ask the angels to cut the cords that bind you to that situation.

In your mind, say: 'I release everything that no longer serves my purpose. I am free.'

Once you've felt the weight of all that's held you back come off your shoulders, hug your parent. Surround both of you in loving light. Know in your heart that you truly forgive and you are truly forgiven for all past hurts.

You can now say: 'I am healed. You are healed. We are healed.'

Chapter 12
THOSE WE HAVE LOST

I'm very much aware that people often seek me out in times of almost unbearable sadness. These are times when I'm blessed to be able to pass on messages of comfort and support.

I remember a woman called Cathy who visited me when she was going through a very tough time at home. Her marriage was at rock bottom and her self-confidence had hit the floor. As I began her reading, her angels surrounded her and poured light all over her energy, trying to lift the weight she carried on her shoulders.

I asked them what was at the root of all this tension and why Cathy felt everything was hopeless. They told me that she'd miscarried a much-wanted child and couldn't move past her loss. They wanted her to know that she was surrounded by love, but she was unable to see it.

They brought the child's energy forwards. They told me that it was a girl who would have been named Holly. Cathy acknowledged that she'd lost a baby, and when she was told the little one's name, she burst into tears, acknowledging that was indeed the name she'd chosen. Although it was an emotional time, she felt reassured knowing the angels had her beautiful baby in spirit.

While I never underestimate the emotional trauma of a loved one passing to spirit, I believe that the love of the angels and their ability to bring those loved ones back to us through spirit is a powerful way to ensure that we never truly feel loss again.

Recently a lady called Lisa visited me for a reading. She told me that she'd been to see me three years earlier, but I couldn't recall her. We were both interested in finding out whether I would tell her the same things as before or whether it would be different this time.

Angels came in very quickly for her and showed me that she was a strong family-oriented person. They told me of her love for her two sons and that she was very protective of them, especially at the moment. I felt that there was a great deal of pressure on her for some reason and the angels said: 'She is unearthing her past. This is a very emotional time; however, the difficult moments have a purpose. They are for the greater good of all involved.'

Lisa felt that this made sense, but I was unhappy with the cryptic nature of the message.

The angels then showed me Lisa's past and I was totally unprepared for what I witnessed – there was a horrific image of her being abused as a child by her grandfather. I felt that the old man was still alive, which was confirmed when I was told that she was currently involved in a lawsuit against him. The angels told me, 'Lisa is doing this to protect her sons – they can't go through what she went through.'

When I passed on this comment, Lisa agreed with it all. 'My grandfather abused me and others,' she said. 'It has now come full circle and someone has tried to follow in his footsteps.'

Things became very emotional and then a woman called Mina was brought through from spirit by the angels.

'It's my gran,' said Lisa. 'Ask her if she knew this was happening to me.'

I did so and told Lisa, 'Your gran had no idea – she was completely unaware of what was going on and never picked up on any of the signs. She so wishes that she'd known so that she could have protected you.'

The spirit of Lisa's grandmother poured love and support into her granddaughter's heart, wanting her to do what was right in the hope that others could be protected from the same horror. Lisa told me a family member had started to act inappropriately towards children and she was refusing to let it happen. It had to be stopped. The angels encouraged her to stay strong for the family and change this old pattern forever. They showed me that the court case would take place soon and that everything would be sorted. This was a huge release for Lisa, who just wanted it all to be over. She went through the rest of the case in the knowledge that she was supported by her angels.

I was once phoned by a woman called Jackie who wanted to book a private reading, and as soon as we spoke, her angel appeared to me. 'You must read for this woman as soon as possible,' I was told.

Trusting this message, I made sure I booked an appointment for Jackie that week. The angel then told me that I should inform her that everything would be sorted even though she'd been in a lot of distress: 'She may feel that she's had enough, but it will all be resolved.'

Given this early connection, I knew that when Jackie came for her reading, it would be a very intense one. Her angels came in quickly and showed me ongoing arguments between her and other family members. I felt that she was being treated like an outsider and that everyone was picking on her as she was an easy target.

As the reading moved on, I could see spirits waiting to come in. The angels wanted to bring in Jackie's father, Tommy. He was a lovely man who came in with a whisky in his hand. He wanted to share his love for his daughter and send his love to his wife, but I realized that the two women had their differences. In addition to Tommy, there was a woman who was a grandmother figure to Jackie and who also sent her love and support.

The angels told me that Jackie had been assaulted and that her confidence in her own sexuality had been shaken. They wanted to help heal this side of her. I was told: 'She was knocked on the head and then abused.' Jackie confirmed that this had happened. I passed all of this information on as well as the angels' desire to help her. She had to release this part of her life and put it behind her. If she allowed that to happen, positive events would follow.

It was a huge challenge trying to get Jackie into a positive frame of mind. She really felt that she was a bad person and wasn't good enough for anyone or anything. While I was speaking to her, she sat with her hood up covering her face. She couldn't bear to look at herself, never mind allow anyone else to do so.

The angels told me I must help her regain her confidence.

I took Jackie to the mirror in my office and persuaded her to take her hood down. She had such a lovely face. I encouraged her to see how beautiful she was.

As she looked at herself in the mirror, I said: 'The angels want you to love yourself. They believe in you and love you. Your father wants to remind you how much he loved you too. If you can begin to look at yourself in a positive light, others will too. What you have to accept, Jackie, is that no one is against you. You have to release these thoughts that they are. You can do this.'

I asked her to point out something about herself that she liked.

'I like my eyes, I suppose,' she said grudgingly. 'A bit.'

I asked why.

'They're quite a nice colour,' she muttered.

'They're *gorgeous*!' I told her. 'Have you ever seen eyes that are such a deep blue?'

I could see the glimmer of a smile.

'You see, you have wonderful qualities as a soul,' I told her. 'Do you think you deserve love, Jackie?'

She shrugged.

I asked her again.

She shrugged again.

I asked her again. I was gentle, but she knew I wouldn't give up.

'Yes, yes, I do really – deep down,' she finally admitted. It was almost as if she was embarrassed to say the words.

'Then all you have to do is feel it,' I told her. 'Look into your own eyes and say, "You've always done the best you can, Jackie. I love you, Jackie."'

Jackie found this exercise so difficult, but she did it.

Some months later she contacted me saying a lot had come out of the woodwork. It had been hard, she wouldn't deny that, but by focusing on only the good, she'd persevered and listened to her angels. They'd told her that this was a transitional period when blocks and negative energy were being released so that she could move on fearlessly. It was a relief to her to know she was finally on the path to freedom.

One day I conducted a reading for a woman who had many loved ones in the spirit world. The angels brought through her parents, grandparents and many others. They loved this lady, Hilary, as she believed in their existence completely and frequently prayed to them. She told me that I was giving her amazing details, but there was one person she would really like to hear from. I can never promise anything, but I asked the angels for help. I heard the word 'loo' and then Hilary shouted, 'Yes, that's her, it's Lindy Loo!'

The angels brought in a young-at-heart character with a fun-loving personality and the ability to put everyone at ease. She was a friend of Hilary's. I was shown her suffering a great deal before she passed with a cancerous condition which had affected her in the stomach area. Hilary had had some difficulty seeing her in her final days and Lindy Loo wanted her to know that she was holding nothing against her. She kept showing me a black poodle called Cassie. It seemed that Hilary was now caring for the dog and Lindy Loo was delighted that her pet and her friend were together and caring for each other.

Sometimes it's so nice to have quite straightforward sessions – and then I remind myself what it is I'm actually doing and wonder how I've got to the stage where I can think of angel conversations as 'straightforward'!

I went to a house recently to visit a woman I'll call Theresa. Her house was busy and she had two other friends over for readings too. Reading for her friends in the kitchen, one at a time, I felt it was a great and successful night of love and communication, but for me there wasn't a huge 'wow' factor.

When Theresa came in for her reading I asked her if she'd ever had one before and she said she'd had many readings from other local mediums.

I put my hands on top of hers and instantly saw a horrible memory of her being abused as a child. It was one of the most vivid visions I've ever seen in my career and my eyes filled with tears and pain.

Surprised by the look in my eyes, Theresa asked if I was alright. I told her I was, but that I knew her life had been filled with abusive relationships from early childhood onwards and that was what she'd seen on my face. The angels told me that the fear of abuse had been present throughout Theresa's life and been expressed in self-harm.

Theresa revealed her arms to me. They were covered with cuts and slashes. It was shocking to see.

'We want to tell her that love exists in her life,' said the angels, 'especially with her five children. One of her sons has joined us in heaven and is ready to speak to his mother.'

A young man of about 20 came into the room. I felt that he hadn't been in heaven too long and obviously knew that he'd passed before his time. He told me his name – let's say Kevin. He and his mum had had a rocky relationship and I was shown their arguments.

'Mum, I want you to know I forgive you,' Kevin said. 'I now understand why you couldn't love us properly.'

Upon hearing her son's words, Theresa became terribly upset, so I asked her if she was sure that she wanted to continue. Holding my hand, she nodded.

Kevin went on, 'Mum, I know that you were abused as a child and that's why you filled your life with drugs and alcohol, to pretend it didn't happen.'

Taking deep breaths, we continued.

The angels told me, 'The boy and his mother didn't speak before he passed and this is why she is filled with so much guilt in her life right now. Knowing she is forgiven will help her heart to heal.'

The angels wanted to acknowledge that Theresa had stopped using alcohol and drugs to mask her feelings and was ready for counselling. The fear of loss had affected her life so much that her kids were under the watchful eyes of social services, who checked regularly that she was a fit mother. She said that she'd nothing to hide from anyone and just wanted to do well for the rest of her kids. Although the loss of her son was a heavy burden, she felt motivated to keep strong for her family. That night, she learned that she wasn't alone, she had support from the other side, and angels were with her son, rooting for her recovery.

Theresa wanted to speak to her son. She wanted him to know that she was sorry for how she'd behaved and how low she'd felt since his passing. His energy surrounded her and the lights in the room even flickered as we spoke.

'He is with you now,' I said, 'and always will be. He loves you and you'll always be his mum.'

The angels stepped back in and asked if Theresa was ready to clear the abusive patterns that she'd allowed to dominate her life. It turned out that she'd always been in abusive relationships and had been beaten up by boyfriends numerous times – it didn't matter who it was, every single one of them had done the same thing to her, and she had lost all faith in men.

When she agreed to go back into the pattern and look at it, I saw that her mother had hated men too. I saw Theresa as a small child with her mother constantly saying, 'All men are untrustworthy arseholes!' Because it was her mother saying the words, Theresa had believed them without question. So the pattern had been laid down for her.

Her mother had still been saying the same old thing some years later, when Theresa had been abused and brutally raped by a neighbour. He had threatened to kill her if she told anyone. Fearing for her life, Theresa had kept it all quiet, but the horror of the abuse had remained with her. She'd always been afraid it was going to happen again, and that she was going to be rejected or treated badly – and so she had been. The fear had attracted horrible relationships into her life and left her in the state she was in right now.

The angels and I worked tirelessly together to take her back to her childhood. I asked her to look back at herself then. She saw a child who felt unloved and unsafe. Her inner child still felt that way. We decided to change that. Theresa imagined her beautiful inner child being wrapped up in pink energy which was safe and strong.

She said to her inner child, 'I'm sorry for not speaking up sooner,' and the inner child replied, 'I forgive you.'

This was a huge relief to Theresa. She was beginning to forgive herself.

So much had gone on in the reading and I decided we'd done enough work for that session. Theresa felt in touch with her son in spirit again; she knew she was loved and deserved love in her life. I gave her positive mind affirmations and prayers, including a prayer to Archangel Michael, so she could focus on only the good in her life. The angels encouraged her to continue working with a counsellor and get the things out that needed to be out, including all of her anger and resentment. While she did this, she could continue to work with them on self-forgiveness.

Once our session was over, I told Theresa I wanted to change the way she viewed men. We're not all users! I told her to keep the money for the session because she could use it for a treat for her four kids instead. She was surprised and tried to give it to me anyway, but I insisted.

Although Theresa is still working through her issues, I continue to send the light of angels to her in the hope she finds her inner light.

Supported by Angels

All of us face challenging issues at some point in our life. One thing with angels is, if they can't get us out of a situation, they'll support us through it. If a difficult situation has been created as a lesson for us to overcome, then they'll be with us all the way.

Angels can also help us do the right thing at the right time. So many of us question ourselves and wonder whether we're doing the right thing. Angels encourage us to trust the flow of life and our own intuition. Our intuition is a powerful force and I believe a lot of the time it is guided by our angels.

If you're unsure as to whether you're doing the right thing at any time, you can use the technique I've already given you for making the connection with angels (*see page 26-7*) or ask them to point you in the right direction using signs (*see page 129*).

You can also say: 'Thank you, angels, for being with me now and directing me on the path that is right for me.'

If everything begins to run more smoothly than before, then you're definitely on the right path. You may also feel your solar plexus guiding you, as if there's an invisible rope pulling you in a certain direction.

If you feel the opposite, if your stomach feels swollen and you're just not getting through something easily, if things are going wrong left, right and centre, stop and hold back. Always follow your signs and directions – we call this divine guidance – and the angels will guide you to happiness.

Chapter 13

A BELIEF IN THE LIGHT

People often ask whether there are bad angels. Perhaps it's because we often think pretty harsh things about ourselves that we wonder whether angels too have a dark side.

The work that I am privileged to do has very few concrete answers – it's a world of light and shade – but this is one enquiry that I can reply to categorically: never, ever, have I had any issues with, or seen, a bad angel. Many people would argue that to have light, you must have darkness. Although that makes sense in so much of life, it simply does not apply to angels.

While there are no bad angels, I have had to address the issue of whether 'bad' people have angelic support. I'd like to take this opportunity to outline some of my own personal beliefs relating to spirit and angelic support, which I accept may be difficult for those unfamiliar with this way of thinking to accept.

I believe that 'bad' people do have angels – angels can't decide if we're going to be negative people or not. We all are put on this Earth and we all choose our path, and the angel we are given at birth is ours no matter what. Angels won't support any dark or destructive act a person performs, but neither can they intervene; they have to step back and watch it happen.

However, I also believe that the universe works in mysterious ways. Sometimes bad things create certain situations or learning experiences in the world which we must work to overcome together. Our purpose on Earth, and in life, is to grow as a soul, and sometimes we have to go through disastrous situations, or even create them, in order to grow.

Anna was a girl of about 20 who opened the door to me when I turned up to do a series of readings at a house in Greenock. As I walked up the stairs, the spirit outline of a man in dark grey bumped into me. The feeling was as if someone had put their fingers into my brain and my stomach. It was horrible. I closed my eyes and asked for my angels to surround me in light to protect me from any dark presences in the home.

At that point Kamael appeared to me and said: 'We're not here for long, friend, and there's a reason for your visit. Bear with us. There will be some changes to the energy around you, but you can go home shortly.'

I trust my angels more than anything, so went along with the evening just as I would normally.

When the first girl came in for her reading, I said, 'This house has had bother with spirits, hasn't it?'

She replied that it had, but that no other psychic had ever noticed. I found that odd; it was so clear to me.

The girl sat down for her reading. A lady spirit came into the room and made an audio link with me, saying, 'My name is Mary and I'm looking to speak to Mary.'

I asked the girl whether there was someone in the house with that name. She said there was, but she wasn't scheduled for a reading.

'This is the reason you are here, Kyle,' Kamael told me. 'You are not to do readings in this house, but to speak to her.'

'I'll need to speak to her if possible,' I said, 'even if she isn't planning on having a reading. Angels have told me that I can't do readings in this house but I must speak to Mary if she's willing.'

A few moments later a dark-haired lady entered the room. She was slim and smiling and seemed quite excited that I'd called her in. I found out that she was the owner of the house.

The spirit of Mary came through again and the Mary with me confirmed that it was her aunt. I was then told to tell her, 'Ryan is safe. He is here in heaven.'

The lady seemed shocked by the information. I then saw her in Ireland and felt that was an important connection. This was followed by an image of a baby in an incubator in hospital, with wires all around it. I described what I'd seen.

Mary said, 'That's Ryan, my son. I lost him not long after giving birth to him in Ireland.'

While I was talking to Mary, the spirit present in the home was still trying to torment me, but I could feel another spirit fighting it off. It was like something from an exaggerated thriller movie.

The spirit who was keeping the darker presence at bay was called Isobel. Mary confirmed that this was her mother. It became apparent that she was coming through to tell Mary she was looking after her and trying to keep the haunting spirit away. She just wanted her daughter to know that all was well where she was now, and also that she was protecting her from lower energies.

Mary told me she'd been tormented for many years by an unseen presence in her home. It would make noises, produce foul smells and even pin her down at times. Since the passing of her mother, it seemed to have stopped, though.

Giving Mary the evidence that her son Ryan was in heaven with her aunt and mother was most satisfying and really made the hairs stand up on my skin. As I was closing up, I looked at my arm and saw a tattoo on it which spelled 'Ryan'. Mary confirmed that her partner had recently got such a tattoo – evidence only she could have known.

There's no doubt in my mind that we are the creator of our own life and sometimes we unconsciously create illness and disease by the way we think.

I was recently contacted by a man named Gerry who booked for a reading with me at my office. In he walked, a man in his early sixties, his hair dyed to a light brown colour, and began telling me that the last psychic he'd seen had been rubbish and nothing had come true! He then proceeded to hand me a piece of paper.

'What's this?' I asked.

'The questions I want answered!' he replied sternly.

I was shocked that he was willing to reveal information to me at this stage by telling me the questions he wanted me to focus on.

'Do you mind if I put these out of the way?' I said, placing the piece of paper on a shelf.

I prefer not to know anything about anyone until I've made a link with the angels. I had to explain to Gerry that I wasn't a fortune-teller and didn't like to predict too much, as I preferred to help my clients create the wellbeing they desired.

After doing so, I tuned into Gerry's angels and could see energy swirling around him in clashing colours of red and green.

'You're a really stubborn man, Gerry, and I don't even think you see it!' I said.

He smiled and waited for more.

The angels stepped in: 'Tell Gerry we're here to help him achieve optimum health again. We also want him to know his son Tony is here to speak. When his son passed, Gerry blamed himself because his son was on his own at the time. But Tony was his own worst enemy. While here on Earth, he was influenced by alcohol and smoked drugs.'

Gerry confirmed this was all true. I could see that Tony was a changed man now, though.

'Your features are very like his, Gerry,' I said, 'especially with that square jawline and forehead, although his hair was much darker than yours.' He nodded at all of this. 'Please know Tony is well and with you.'

'Gerry's two other children are still on Earth,' said the angels. 'One of his questions is about his elder daughter.

She's a nurse who never seems to stop working. This is why her marriage failed – it lost passion.'

Gerry was amazed. He told me that one of his questions was: 'Why did my daughter's marriage fail?' And the other question was: 'Is my son alright and does he forgive me?'

The angels continued: 'Gerry is very determined at this time to continue working; however, the universe has offered him time to heal himself.'

'I want to know why I have blood in my urine,' Gerry snapped.

I explained that I wasn't a medical expert, but with his permission we could look into why this was happening from a mental and spiritual point of view. He agreed to it.

'It's because he's pissed off with his ex-wife,' I was told. 'He's never forgiven her!'

'Does that make sense, Gerry?' I asked.

'Yes!' he said. 'I can't forgive her for taking my home and all my money. Now all I'm left with is a £5,000 legal bill and I just don't want to pay it.'

The angels encouraged Gerry to work on forgiveness because if he could do so, the issue surrounding his urine would clear up. He must do this before they turned into something worse, they said.

'I've already got cysts around my prostate and they don't know how to get rid of them,' Gerry admitted.

'Well, there's your answer,' I said.

The angels also told me he had the money to pay the legal bill – he was just refusing to do it. He admitted this was the case.

Like many people, Gerry resisted things he didn't like or didn't want to accept. He had created the medical problems with his own mind because he wasn't willing to release his anger. This was his opportunity to forgive and become a stronger soul.

Gerry emailed me not long after the reading to ask about a self-help book I'd recommended on forgiveness. This told me he was ready to forgive, let go and move on.

All sorts of people come to me for readings. I try not to judge anyone. If I can help someone, I will.

I was once invited to a home to conduct a reading for a young couple. The young woman had lost two children to heaven and wanted to know that they and other loved ones were alright. The angels produced some fantastic evidence for her, including the names and ages of these child spirits and whom they were with. I was overjoyed, but I felt that I'd actually been sent to that home for another reason.

Then the woman's partner, Joe, came in for a reading. He was in his early twenties, wearing a tracksuit and sporting a black eye. I thought, 'Oh dear, here we go...!'

Joe sat down and I shook his hand.

'So, have you ever had this done before then?' I asked.

'Aye, I got it done at the carnival,' he replied, gruffly.

'Well, I work differently,' I explained, 'but we'll see what comes through.'

I knew Joe was a troublemaker and I had to watch what I said and think about how I was going to put things across. However I could also see that Joe had an angel beside him wanting him to do well.

The aura around the top right-hand shoulder of a person seems to represent the parents who are in their life, and Joe's was bright red. I instinctively knew this represented his mother, as his father wasn't in his life. The red haze around Joe's shoulder showed that she was opinionated and strong-minded.

'She doesn't put up with any nonsense at all, does she?' I said. He laughed. I continued, 'The angels have told me that they've been around you recently and they want to help you make more of your life. They know you've been in and out of police cars on two occasions in the last month.'

Joe smirked.

'I'm not here to judge you,' I went on, 'and quite frankly, I don't want to know what you've done, but you must know that there are people who believe in you on Earth and in heaven. They want you to do well for your family.'

'He can change it all,' said the angels. 'With the recent opportunities in work, we are guiding this man to a better future. There will be a court case in the next few weeks where he will have to pay a fine – this is his chance to move on and leave this life behind him.'

Again all of this was true.

Now I had to tell Joe a few home truths: 'I have to say that, on top of this, there have been some dodgy dealings that you know you don't have to be attached to.'

'It's all he knows,' a voice said. I looked up and saw a tall slim man with glasses standing behind Joe. His teeth were missing and he was smoking what seemed to be a joint.

'Who are you?' I asked.

'Tell him that John's here,' came the reply.

The young man was pleased and said, 'That's my stepdad. He taught me everything I know!'

John became almost overpowering and said, 'You need to get out of this, wee man! You need to avoid Steven, you can't trust him.'

At that point I asked the angels to step in. I wasn't about to be stuck in the middle of a judgemental discussion.

'Tell this young man that John watches over his daughter and wants your mum to know that he does forgive her and still loves her now,' they said.

It transpired that John had fallen out with Joe's mum the day before he'd passed from a drug overdose.

'Do you feel you know what's right and wrong for you?' I asked Joe.

'Yeah, mate, yeah,' he replied. 'I'm going to work hard at being a dad for my family's sake. I'm ready to leave this all behind me.'

He seemed to be genuine.

'Promise yourself, Joe,' I said, 'because you do deserve a good life. Risky deals won't get you anywhere – in fact, you'll just dig yourself into an even deeper hole if you keep on this way.'

'I'm ready for a fresh start,' he declared.

John's energy faded into the background and Joe told me that it was true about Steven – he often told on everyone else to protect himself. I encouraged Joe to act compassionately and just let go of Steven so he didn't have more rubbish to pick up. I only hope he listened to me and the angels – it was a huge opportunity for him to turn things around.

Sending Love to a Situation

Whatever the situation, it can be made worse by thinking of it in a particular way. If something has happened that you are concerned about, don't worry. Instead of allowing it to drag you down, you can surround it with the love of angels.

All you have to do is imagine the situation (in the past, present or future), any people involved, yourself and anything else involved being surrounded by light. I often surround things in pink light because it reminds me of love. That is a good colour to use in any situation.

You can then say: 'Thank you, angels, for surrounding my situation in light and resolving it now.'

When you do this, you step back from it, allowing the light of the angels to surround it.

Trust with all your might that the angels will help.

Remember that angels can only intervene when you aren't surrounding a situation with fear, as they cannot penetrate fear. By surrounding it with light and passing it over to them through affirmative prayer, you will definitely give it a more positive energy.

If you begin to worry about it at any point, just surround the situation in golden and pink energy. Gold represents the divine and pink represents love, so together they represent divine love. That way you know the situation is being looked after by divine angels.

Chapter 14

ALWAYS THERE, ALWAYS WATCHING

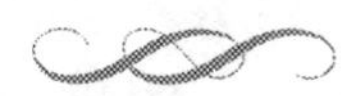

One of the most exciting things I've ever done is write a newspaper column. I was so lucky to be given the opportunity. Many people write in to me now, asking for help and often giving very little information – which suits me fine, as I don't need it, I have angels to help me!

One lady wrote to me on two separate occasions but used different names. Very few people actually get their letters printed, due to the enormous mailbag I receive and the pressure of space, but, oddly, this woman, Lucy, saw her words in print twice. Her sister, Anne, then booked a reading with me anonymously, after which she confirmed everything I'd already said!

When Anne came for her reading, it was a beautiful summer's evening and we sat at the window in my living room with the window open and a breeze wafting through. As soon as Anne sat down, angels connected to me and I knew there was a lot to speak about. The angels told me about a family dispute which had resulted in a big falling-out. There had been animosity over money and the possession of a home.

The angels encouraged Anne to lie low at this time and focus only on the best. They told me that she'd recently been bereaved and there was a spirit who wanted to express his gratitude towards her.

They brought in a man and said, 'Billy's here.'

Anne began to cry. Billy had been her uncle. She'd been very close to him and had cared for him to his dying day.

'Billy wants Anne to know that he left her the house and that she's to have it,' the angels said. 'The legal documents state that, so she should not question it.'

'This is what I wanted to know!' Anne cried out. She'd been given such a hard time since Billy had passed because he'd left her his home. Other members of his family had objected to his will, but she'd been his nurse and this was his thanks.

In the two readings the angels also made me aware that Anne's car had been vandalized. They told me it had been someone who worked with cars daily, so knew what they were doing when it came to tampering with it. To my horror, this was true – the engine of her car had been disconnected by a relative who worked as a mechanic.

The angels encouraged Anne to send love to all involved. They assured her that things would then begin to change.

I've since had correspondence from both Anne and Lucy and both have confirmed that things are now getting much better.

In another case, I received two pleas in the same mailbag from members of the same family, one a daughter and the other a wife. How I picked these two random letters out of a bag of hundreds baffles me to this day. My actions were clearly guided by angels – it was a message that desperately needed to be passed on.

Both letter-writers asked me not to disclose their names because they didn't want to upset each other. The daughter's letter read:

I am writing this letter to you while looking at my dad's Order of Service from his funeral.

He suddenly and most tragically took his own life four weeks ago. For what reason I do not know; as far as I know there were no money worries and no depression.

I miss my dad terribly and cannot accept what he has done. I was a daddy's girl and just cannot come to terms with it. He was a deep person and a private person. My wee boy was his pride and joy, his best friend. I'm torturing myself wondering what I could have done to prevent this – more so, the answers I have to give to my wee boy.

I hope he is at rest.

I love him so much and am finding it hard to let go. Please help me in some way. It will be a blessing if this gets published, as I can put it in my remembrance box for my wee boy, Murray.

This was my reply:

> *I am very sorry for this loss in your life.*
>
> *I can see it has hit the family hard, as it would anyone, and I am sending you extra angels to help heal your hearts.*
>
> *I want to say that it is too early for me to get the best communication from your father; however, I was very drawn to write, as you were not the only family member who wrote to me about him.*
>
> *I feel your father in spirit; he is healing himself and his emotions. His biggest issue in life was communicating his feelings – he never knew how to express himself as best as he could. It is important to say he is settling down and just keeps apologizing for the mess he left behind.*
>
> *I want you to know that he wants you to know he is with you forever and that he will be watching from above. He sends his vibes to your mother and is sending her positivity and help to overcome this situation.*
>
> *I want you to connect with other family members and pull together as a unit; you can all help each other. Light a candle at a window and tell your dad all your feelings and fears and release any anger you have on your chest. It's important for you to grieve and let all your emotions out; once you do this, you will see the light at the end of your tunnel. Dad will be watching and guiding.*

As for Murray, he sees him and knows there have been so many questions you can't answer. He will see his grandfather in dreams or spirit form. His grandfather will let him know he is well and still watching him. He wants to talk of the special 'badge' and talks about the name 'James'.

Your father is sorry and is helping you move on. It is unethical for us to ask the spirit world why people have taken their own life, so I will be unable to answer this for you, but I wish you well.

Some time later, I was in the back room of a building where I sometimes provide readings when I heard the owner tell a woman that I was there. This woman had written the other letter I'd picked out of my mailbag. She said that she'd been drawn to the shop that day, but didn't know why, and would like to meet me. It was then that she confirmed everything I'd said. The 'special badge' had been a little thistle she had pinned to her husband's suit jacket before they'd closed the casket and James was a family member in heaven. She was astounded that I'd known so much from just the few words she'd written.

I got to know her husband, as a while later he came through again, this time calling himself John. It turned out that the man I was reading for at the time was his son-in-law. John passed on very similar messages to before, in particular messages of comfort to his wife, who was finding it difficult because she'd found him hanging by his neck.

Some months passed and this time John's other daughter came for a reading. I had trouble reading for her. When I asked the angels why, I was told it was because John wanted to speak to his wife. I rebooked the girl to come back with her mother. When I met them at the door of my office, the penny dropped: it was the woman I'd met in the shop a whole year earlier! It was time for her to receive her communication.

In the reading we cleared up so much information and she felt hugely loved by her angels. From that point, she found it much easier to move on. It wasn't easy for this lovely woman, but she knew her husband was settled and fine now.

Every week I receive hundreds of letters from people who read my column and features on angels. I'm also very much involved in the music world, but realized some time ago that everyone is treated equally by angels, no matter whether they're a celebrity or not.

I once did a reading for a young woman called Shaz, who was a very open-minded soul with great energy. Her heart was pulsing with good energy and there was a true light about her. Her aura was golden and bright.

After describing her warm, welcoming and independent character, the angels brought in the presence of a lady from spirit. She was a small Indian woman who smiled a lot. She was a very spiritual soul herself, which I knew from the gold emanating from her aura.

I heard 'Joshi' or something similar, but Shaz couldn't place the name. I said to my angels, 'Please get the name right so that we can confirm to this lady that there's life after life.' I then heard 'Baboji' which she confirmed was what she called her grandmother.

The spirit then showed me a mental picture of Shaz being dressed from head to toe in red. I felt I was at a wedding.

I said, 'Your grandmother never got to your wedding, did she?'

Shaz said she hadn't.

'You wanted her to be there and she wants to say she was with you. She says that you incorporated red into your outfit to acknowledge your Indian roots, didn't you?'

'Yes, that's correct. I had a white wedding dress with red extras,' said Shaz.

'Your Baboji was with you and said you were beautiful,' I went on, as tears filled Shaz's eyes.

I then saw a pearl in my mind. It turned out that Shaz had worn her grandmother's pearl at her wedding. This was another reminder for her that there was an everlasting love surrounding her.

The angels surrounded Shaz with light and explained that she felt unsettled in her home. They told me that there were also unresolved issues with her parents. They then showed me Kingston-upon-Thames, southwest of London, which Shaz confirmed was her birthplace.

The angels said: 'She's not entirely happy in Scotland. A return south would be good and "on-Sea" will be important.'

Shaz's face lit up. 'You're joking!' she exclaimed. We've been desperate to move to Clacton-on-Sea for a good few years now!'

The angels then told me: 'Shaz is a teacher and she has a really good way with the children. She is very gifted. It is important that she follows her life role as a teacher but is open to receiving new opportunities. We will guide her to where she needs to be. It will be near where she has felt drawn to.'

Shaz was overjoyed at the thought of moving to near Clacton-on-Sea and the fact that she would continue her work as a primary school teacher. The angels gave her positive mind work to create her move to her dream home. She said she felt a huge weight had been lifted from her shoulders and her faith in the afterlife had been restored.

Chapter 15
DIVINE CHARACTERS

I always urge people to remember that angels are divine in character – they are not judgmental in any way whatsoever and they don't bear grudges. They differ in personality and in purpose, but they are all beings of love. It is important to remember that they work under the spiritual laws of the universe, so if something is set to happen, it will, but even if angels can't change a situation, they will support us through it.

One evening, I was booked to do readings for four members of one family. With the first, the mother, I had difficulties. This was unusual and I apologized profusely. But with the next person, the eldest daughter, the same thing happened. Not only was this very odd, but I was also being enveloped by a feeling of overwhelming sadness which wasn't linked to the fact that the readings weren't 'working'; there was something making me feel that I should just give up and leave. I actually said to the family that they should get another psychic, as I was getting no messages at all, and I went home.

Two months later I bumped into the youngest daughter of the family, who recognized me. Again I apologized for what had happened, but when the girl said that her father had died a few weeks after the failed readings, I realized that this had been the problem.

Angels can't change what is set in stone and I now realized my angels had been protecting me and my reputation, as I always refuse to foretell someone's passing. I firmly believe that a psychic's job is to provide evidence, guidance and insight, not pass on messages of doom and bereavement.

It is the role of angels to help us whatever's going on in our life, but if we've created particular circumstances in order to learn, or our journey here on Earth has ended, then they can only support us through what is happening. But if we face a life-threatening situation when it's not our time to go, angels can save us.

I was recently consulted by a woman called Nyree, who'd been absolutely lost in her life since the passing of her partner some time before. Though she came to hear evidence from her partner, it was the angels who led the reading for her.

At that point Nyree was using alcohol to hide the pain of her loss and the fear of rejection in her life. She found herself in financial difficulty and plummeted into a hole of deep despair.

She believed in angels and a higher power, but failed to ask for help or assistance. She just sat there feeling depressed, which was leading her nowhere.

In the consultation, the angels surrounded Nyree in brilliant golden light and emphasized that they wanted her to see herself in a much better light. They told me that she continually said, both out loud and in her mind, 'Why is no one helping me?' They were really trying to ask her, 'Why aren't you helping yourself?'

Nyree surrounded herself in fear, despair and chemicals from the drugs prescribed by her GP, which the angels, with their high vibrational energy, couldn't penetrate. She had to learn this one for herself.

There was no doubt that Nyree wanted help. One day she'd been reading the paper in a coffee shop when she'd seen my page. It had called out to her, she'd felt drawn to me and when she met me, she said it was if she already knew me.

Through me, her angel said to her, 'We want you to know that although you didn't choose your husband's passing, you've had the choice of how to act since. We're willing to assist you in changing your life, but first you must take back your power.'

The angel was talking about something we all must realize – we are in control of our lives and if we focus on depressing thoughts and feelings then we're only going to find ourselves in depressing situations. But angels want us to focus on things that are positive in nature.

As I was told all this, a soft voice said, 'Like her glorious daughter.'

I looked up to see a beautiful golden angel with long hair which was moving in an unseen wind. The pale angel's feet were off the ground; she had the most beautiful wings holding her in the air. When I asked, 'What's your name?' she responded sweetly, 'Sophia. I am Nyree's guardian angel.'

Nyree's face lit up. 'My daughter *is* glorious! She is so talented and strong. The weirdest thing about it is that her confirmation name is Sophia too!'

I believe this was the angels trying to get the message to Nyree that there was light out there for her, but because she'd been drawn in by her depression, it had never filtered in.

From this point Nyree was keen to know more about angels and how she could improve her light with their help. I asked her whether she prayed, and she said that she'd thought about it but never really done it. I gave her affirmative prayers and her angel's name. Now she was ready to start making her life better. She felt encouraged to let go of alcohol and stand on her own two feet.

I've since heard from her family that Nyree has stopped drinking, has begun to face her issues with debt and regularly uses angel cards for guidance. Through the love of angels, she is moving into a better way of life.

A few months ago, I was conducting readings for a group of girls in their twenties. I have to be honest here – I was worried when I arrived because the building had boarded-up windows and there were some shady-looking characters hanging round outside. I tried to remember the importance of compassion and went inside!

A flood of angels came through – it was beautiful. The girl who lived there with her mother was having some difficulties with her life and work, but her reading went really well. She was told by her angels not to give up after being mistreated in her workplace and initiating a lawsuit.

'She must follow the case through,' they said. 'This is one of her first lessons: she must see that she deserves the best.'

I asked them to elaborate on this.

'Her father has split from her mother,' I was told, 'and ceased all communication with her. She feels rejected and has lost faith in humanity.'

As I continued the reading, the angels surrounded the girl with support. They also presented a tiny little kitten to her from spirit and the letters 'TI' came into my head.

'Is it Tina?' I asked.

She began to cry. 'No,' she wept, 'it's Tia, my kitten. I found her dead when I came in from work one day. I'm so glad she's alright.'

My next reading there was for her friend Victoria. Victoria was a nice girl who was very down to earth; I could tell she didn't put up with any nonsense, so I knew I had to do this right. As soon as she walked in, I saw a huge angel to her left and a smiling man to her right. He was holding a baby.

After explaining what I do, I asked for guidance. The angel said, 'Victoria lost her child to heaven three weeks ago. We are here to tell her all is well and the child will return to her soon.'

Victoria was surprised by the accuracy of the information that had kicked in before she'd even sat down!

'Tell her Granddad Tommy is here,' said the angels. 'Thomas heard Victoria praying to make sure her baby's soul was safe in heaven, and he did just that.'

A sense of relief came over Victoria. The angels went on, 'This may not be the right time for Victoria to be a mother, but she will be one day – she must know this.' They mentioned her boyfriend by name: 'Stephen has shown huge support for Victoria. We believe they are a match.'

Victoria was happy with what she'd received and didn't want to ask any questions. Although the reading was short, the message was definitely sweet.

Sometime later I was in another house doing readings in a completely different area when Tommy came back to me. I remembered him straight away because of his cheeky smile and happy-go-lucky character.

I said to the woman I was reading for, 'You don't know a girl called Vicky, do you? I see a man called Tommy behind you and he still has her child with him, the one I saw in another reading.'

The woman's jaw dropped in complete amazement. 'Vicky is my daughter!' she said. 'Tommy is my father-in-law! I'm so happy you told me this – it has completely proven to me that this is all real!'

Tommy made a third appearance in one of my readings, this time in a completely different town and to a gentleman. I didn't know what to do, so I decided to tell the man about him.

'That really sounds like my father,' he said, 'but I'll only believe he's there if you tell me his name.'

I told him it was Tommy and he was stunned.

'That's my dad,' he said.

'I know him!' I laughed. 'He pops up a lot – I've read for your daughter and your wife and he's become a bit like my chum in heaven.'

The man laughed and was comforted to learn that his father was so active in watching over his family from above.

I'll never forget the time I was speaking at an event in Dundee and a young woman came over to speak to me. She seemed excited about the prospect of angels and intrigued by my work. I invited her to my free talk later that afternoon where she could see a demonstration of my work and learn more about angels. When I did the talk, though, I couldn't see her anywhere. I was disappointed, because she seemed like a good soul and I wanted her to learn about angels.

Soon after my talk had ended, I went back to the main hall and there she was, looking flustered. She explained that the organizers hadn't let her into the room for health and safety reasons, as the talk had been completely full.

'I went for a reading with someone else instead,' she told me, 'but you'll not believe what he said – he told me there were demons around me.'

I was completely flabbergasted by this information and encouraged her to come and sit beside me.

I asked her, 'Did he tell you anything evidential? Did he prove to you this was true?'

She told me that he'd given her a general reading but had kept referring to a 'negative' being surrounding her. I decided to do a quick check in with the angels about this situation.

The angels told me that there wasn't anything negative around her at all. They added that her son was a dreamer who often saw angels. They also put me in a hairdresser's seat and I could see the girl cutting my hair.

'You're a hairdresser then,' I stated.

'How do you know that?' she asked.

'Well, the angels told me, just like they told me there's no negative energy around you to worry about,' I confirmed.

The one thing that I think the other medium may have got confused by was that there was a younger male spirit in heaven who had been in the girl's life and had passed through tragic circumstances. There was a lot of negativity around his passing and this was maybe where he was getting it from. I gave all of this information to her.

She was shocked and told me that her best friend's partner had taken his own life just a week before. It had left her friend devastated and lost.

The angels told me: 'He isn't ready to come through yet, but he's safe in heaven.'

The girl was so pleased with what I'd given her, but it could all have turned out so differently if she'd been left with nothing but a message that she was surrounded by demons.

Emergency Angels

The best way to contact angels is through affirmative prayer. However, they have also shown me another great way to draw their energy to us, especially in times of need.

Whenever we see 'I am' and then a word, we draw the energy of that word into our being. For example, when we affirm, 'I am the light,' we connect to all things divine and something angels call 'the I am-ness,' which is the true us, our divine spark, our soul.

We can also use an angel's name to bring their divine qualities to us. One that I've often used in times of need is 'I am Michael.' That draws Archangel Michael's energy to me. Michael's energy is especially good when we're in a dangerous situation, a heated discussion or in need of a boost in confidence. It wraps us in his ray of support.

Another excellent one is 'I am Raphael', which calls on the healing angel. If you practise hands-on healing or are overcoming a disease, this will be great for you.

If you're having an argument with a loved one, 'I am Raguel' will help you. Remember, Raguel's name means 'Friend of God' and he is the family angel who resolves all conflicts.

'I am Gabriel' will bring the nurturing, creative energy of Gabriel to you. Gabriel helps us communicate openly with wisdom and power. She is also the angel of mothers, so if you need guidance with your child or children, she can help you with this too.

'I am Uriel' will bring light to your situation – Uriel is the angel of light who inspires us in everything we do. If you're lost and don't know what to do next, his energy will direct you with ease.

You can try this with any angel name. You'll find it makes a remarkable difference to your life.

Chapter 16

AN ANGELIC BONUS

By this point, I hope I've convinced you that each and every single one of you has a guardian angel. However, I've met some people who are even luckier – they have more than one.

One such person was Miranda, a lawyer with two distinctive angels, one who dealt with her work and another who represented her creative side. The professional angel encouraged her only to work for the good of humanity, and the creative angel, who was her personal guardian angel, was keen to encourage her to develop that side of her life. This was an unusual angelic combination. Both angels wanted to show Miranda the importance of balance; as a divorce lawyer, she was finding that the experiences she had at work were affecting her personal life and she was finding it hard to commit to a relationship.

The reading was absolutely amazing. Miranda loved her job, but it did sometimes make her lose faith in humanity. She loved people, but was very solitary. The angels said that they wanted to inspire her to believe in people again. If she lost hope entirely, this would attract more negative cases and people into her life. She needed a more positive focus so that the universe could deliver easier situations to her.

'We've brought Miranda here not only to help her discover her faith in humanity again but because there's also a spirit who desperately wants to thank her from the other side,' the angels told me.

The spirit of a younger woman with short hair entered the room. The angels told me her name was Maggie.

'Do you know who this is?' I asked.

Miranda said that she did.

'She keeps showing me an envelope and I can't help but feel she wants to discuss an important letter,' I added.

Miranda said this was correct and the angels contributed: 'It's what she did with the letter that's important. Maggie is so thankful she helped it reach the rightful owner that she wants to assist her in finding a soul-mate relationship. It will be her way of showing her gratitude.'

Miranda looked relieved. But I had to ask her what the heck was going on because I was so confused!

She then told me that Maggie was a friend of her best friend, Helen. She'd suffered from cancer for many months before passing peacefully. The settlement of her estate had gone through Miranda's law firm. Although Miranda wasn't dealing with the case directly, she saw most of what was going on with it.

Along with Maggie's will and other things, there was a letter to Helen. It was just a basic thanks and appreciation of the friend that she'd been so fond of, but the family insisted they didn't want to pass it on because it didn't matter now Maggie was 'dead'. Miranda, however, felt an increasing urge to deliver the letter to Helen. She believed – and now knew – that this was Maggie urging her from the other side.

Eventually she couldn't hold back. Even though she was breaking her code of conduct, she knew it was the best thing to do. She photocopied the letter and passed it on to Helen. Helen was overjoyed at receiving the letter from her friend in heaven. To know Maggie had loved her and been grateful for everything she'd done made her feel so whole. It also turned out that Maggie's sister was jealous of the bond Helen had had with her and hadn't wanted to pass on the letter simply out of spite.

Now Maggie was thanking Miranda for passing on the information and saying she would join Miranda's two angels in encouraging her to find faith in humanity again and receive love in her life.

I told Miranda to give humanity a chance. 'You're an amazing soul,' I said. 'You've done so much to heal a soul, both on Earth and in heaven. If you can just see and feel your inner light, you'll allow others to see it too.'

Miranda admitted that she was excited to see what would happen after the reading and said out loud, 'Right, Maggie and angels, I'm ready for a loving relationship!'

She left the reading a new person.

On another occasion, I met a woman called Orla whose son had won a voucher for a reading with me in a charity raffle.

Orla was delightful. When she came into my office, it was as if the room lit up with her inner light. She was surrounded by angels, all committed to her wellbeing and development, and each had a special message for her.

'We've been with Orla since she was a young age,' they said. 'We were with her when she lost her mother as a child and her father couldn't cope. No matter what has been put into her life, Orla has always stayed strong and had faith in God.'

In my mind I saw Orla at the altar of a Catholic church. She was a very strong believer in her religion and I knew that she felt guilty seeing me because of some things the Church said about mediums.

'My readings are very different from those of fortune-tellers,' I reassured her, 'so you needn't worry about doing anything that's against your beliefs. If anything, this reading should strengthen your personal connection with the angels you talk to so much every day.'

Orla told me that not a day went by without her praying to her guardian angel.

The angels took me to a time when Orla had worked as a nurse. She'd been well liked in her job and had loved it very much.

'She often saw angels in her day,' I was told.

Orla confirmed that she'd often seen angels gathering around people's beds when they were ready to move on to the next life.

As the reading progressed, the angels welcomed in Orla's father from heaven. He was dressed as a soldier and had a helmet on. When I told her about this, she said he'd been in the army and been shot in the head but had survived. He'd had metal plates put into his head but had continued his life afterwards.

The angels spoke for him, telling me that he'd been fine after the shooting, but after when her mother had died, he'd never been the same again. He just hadn't been able to cope. He wanted Orla to know he'd always loved her and that he hadn't wanted her to see him unhappy. That's why he'd sent her to stay with relatives in Ireland who'd offer her a much better life.

'And that they did. I was well loved in Ireland. Please tell my daddy I'll always love him,' Orla said, allowing tears of joy to flow at the knowledge that her dad was her loving support from the other side.

The angels continued: 'We want to tell Orla that it was Archangel Michael she met while praying in France.'

Orla gasped. 'I've always wondered about that experience!' she said. 'In church we often speak about angels and people say that they will reveal their name to you. One time I was going to a chapel in France. I went to the gates and they were locked. It was beginning to get dark, as it was winter, and I was worried because I was on my own. As I was shaking the gate with no success, I saw a man beside me. I jumped in surprise, but as I looked at him, I was overwhelmed by the warmth in his face and his smile. He pointed to the far left and said, "Michael." When I looked to the left, I saw another gate. I was glad and turned to thank the man, but he'd disappeared, just vanished into thin air. I walked round to the other entrance and it turned out it was called Saint Michael's Gate. I knew then Archangel Michael had paid me a visit himself.'

The angels continued with guidance for Orla, saying that she had to realize God would not punish her, nor did she have to punish herself for every mistake she'd made.

Orla admitted that her Catholic faith had led her to believe God did punish people.

The angels quickly responded to this: 'God is one word: *love*. The essence of the universe is nothing more. Man can punish man, and man can punish himself, but God will forever love him.'

Orla was able to take this information on board and decided to stop beating herself up when she didn't go to confession or say her Hail Marys – she really did have a pure heart of gold!

I remember one evening when I was doing a presentation on angel communication, I picked a man out of the audience named Martin simply because he had two angels standing with him. They wanted to tell him how proud they were that he'd overcome the worst in his life and had discovered his inner strength and talents. I asked to speak to him after the show to find out more.

In my mind I saw Martin 10 years before as a raging alcoholic with no hope at all. He locked himself inside his home, wouldn't speak to anyone and was literally carrying a lot of weight. Then he believed he was seeing spiritual lights around his home and he turned his life around. The angels told me that the alcohol abuse had been used to hide his natural sensitivity to angels. They were pleased and excited that he was now ready to begin working with them.

This message was a boost of confidence and hope, as Martin now longed to be a spiritual healer and medium working with angels. It seemed he had two angels because when he'd begun his journey he'd been a completely different person from the confident man I'd met that day. The new angel had been awarded to him because he was ready to undertake a new life path.

Martin later came on one of my angel workshops and proved to have a remarkable connection between heaven and Earth. He knew then that this was his calling and his two angels were by his side.

I once conducted a reading for a young girl's 18th birthday. It was bought for her by a family friend who just fancied giving her something different. The girl herself, Siobhan, was so cool. She had dyed red hair and wore square black-rimmed glasses. Her aura was pinkish-red, showing a fiery, hot-headed personality.

At either side of Siobhan there was an angel. They were lanky golden angels with really round faces and piercing black eyes. They didn't talk much, as the spirit of her father was also there, along with a dog, and it was his chance to communicate, but I knew they were there to support this amazing girl. They told me they were her guides and that she'd had a tough time with her parents, so they'd quietly watched over her and made sure she was always strong and determined, which would be her saving grace. By the colour of her aura, there wasn't any doubting that!

The angels told me they were there to supervise a communication from Siobhan's father in heaven. His energy came through and in my mind I saw him as being tipsy.

'Your dad was his own worst enemy and didn't know when to stop drinking,' I told her.

Siobhan was shocked.

'I always loved you, Siobhan,' her father said. 'I'm sorry I broke my promise to get better.'

It seemed he hadn't been able to tear himself away from alcohol, which had eventually been the cause of his lonely passing.

Siobhan began to cry. I knew she'd been terribly close to her father. He began singing 'Wonderwall' to her and she said that was a special song they'd both loved.

Then he stood behind her and a shiver went through her spine. He kept saying, 'Where's your chain? Where's your chain?'

When I passed this on, she replied that she didn't have it on that day but her father had bought her a chain she often clung to, trying to remember her time with him and the bond they shared.

'Your dad loves you, as you know, and will always be with you,' I told her.

Then one of the angels began to talk, saying, 'It's important for Siobhan to work things out with her mother. We want her to know her mum is just looking out for her. She must understand this.'

Siobhan admitted that it'd been some time since she'd spoken to her mother. She'd been living with her gran for months. She and her mum were currently at loggerheads and were as stubborn as each other, but the angels were encouraging her to work things out with her because even though her parents had had a rocky relationship, her dad didn't want her to be without two parents here on Earth.

Siobhan agreed to speak to her mum if her dad would promise he'd be with her in spirit. At that moment, I heard the simple word, 'Always.'

Siobhan was overjoyed – her father was with her and always would be.

Bonus Angels

Any spirits of our family around us, or even another angel, are, in effect, an extra support unit which we must embrace and call forwards if we are to reach our full potential. I refer to these extras as our 'bonus angels'.

I've known many people to have bonus angels with them. A common situation is that when people attune to Reiki or learn a new healing technique, a new angel will join them on their path or work with them for a while until they get the hang of what they're doing. It doesn't mean your guardian angel isn't capable of helping you, but there are many angels, each with their own speciality, just as there are with people here on Earth.

If you haven't been made aware of any bonus angels, don't worry – the angel you have already is more than capable of helping you with your needs. But why not see if you have any bonus angels working with you?

Closing your eyes and taking a deep breath, imagine how many angelic energies are behind you. You may see one, two or even more.

If you're confident enough, use the tuning-in exercise (see page 26-7) *to ask each of them their purpose for being with you and how you can help fulfil that purpose. You can also ask for any messages or any assistance or guidance they can give you. If you breathe deeply as you ask, you will receive guidance.*

Chapter 17

LOVE AND ABUNDANCE

As we come to the end of this journey, I would love every single one of you reading this book to become more aware of your angels, to find whatever you are looking for and to be blessed with love and abundance in all areas of your life.

Love and abundance are waiting for you if you know how to access them and, more importantly, how to recognize that you deserve them. There may be things in your past – people, events, experiences – which make you question this, question who you are or what the future holds for you. I dearly wish you would just put behind you all the negative thoughts, all the beliefs that hold you back, all the things that stop you being the amazing individual you truly are. It's not just what I want; it's what your angels want too.

If you find it difficult to believe in yourself, ask your angels to help you learn to do it. And if you can at this point, trust me. After learning about my experiences and my story, please look on me as a friend, a friend who can help guide you and lead you on this wonderful journey.

Angels won't press you to do anything in your life, nor will they will push you to make changes. You have free will and they recognize this. However, they will encourage you wholeheartedly to seek happiness in your life; they will encourage you to let go of what has held you back. Learning to trust yourself, to release all that has restricted you in the past, to access the help of your guardian angel and to focus on the highest level of existence, will give you the opportunity to realize your desires.

Angels will support us through anything and their teachings are always there for us to tap into. I've learned many things from them. Here are some of them.

Doing vs Being

If there's one thing I've learned about life, it's that we're all on a mission. This mission can take many forms, but we're all searching for something, even if sometimes we're not even aware of the fact.

We're often so busy *doing* that we forget who we are and what we're really here for. We fill our work schedules and social lives up to the hilt. We're constantly on the go. We always tell ourselves that we need to work on the next project, to do this, that and the other, to keep going. We never stop, never slow down.

In Western societies, everything has a label, everything has a name, and many people measure us on what we have and what we do for a living. It's not often we're recognized for who we are as a person, except by some very special individuals.

Life, it would seem, is all about perception. People are constantly trying to work each other out, but in doing so they're missing something very important. The question we need to ask is not who other people are, but who are we?

This is where *being* becomes vitally important. Learning to be at one with yourself is the heart of a happy, fulfilled existence. To do this effectively and appropriately can take a huge change in mindset. So often people will say that they're constantly learning. While this may sound as if it's on the right track, I would add a word of caution: if something negative happens in our life, we'll say it's a learning experience. But what if we're missing the point? What if the lesson wasn't that we had to go through that situation, but that the universe was trying to help us realize something else?

We're Creating Our Own Future

Your life is a reflection of your mind. Your thoughts, both good and bad, are mirrored in what is happening in your life. So, if you can connect with your inner being, if you can find happiness on the *inside*, it will radiate out throughout your life. So stop searching – happiness is already inside you. All you have to do is learn to tap into it. And angels can help you.

I bet there's one phrase you've used at some point in your life: 'mind over matter'. If you've said these words, you've already acknowledged that you have power over physical constraints or challenges.

To take this a step further, I'd suggest that you ask yourself where your mind is. You might automatically point towards your head or think that your mind is connected to your brain, but you'd be wrong. While matter is basically everything you can see, touch and know to be physical, your mind consists of your inner intelligence, your inner genius – it is the real you.

At the moment of conception, you started your journey inside your mother's womb as a double strand of DNA. Your DNA separated 50 times to create 100 trillion cells, which then began your creation. Your body is a remarkable composition of energy. Your cells are said to do six trillion things a second and they all know what every other cell is doing at the same time. Your body is absolutely phenomenal. Just think – it can digest food, play an instrument and create a baby all at the same time! But it gets better – your body tracks the movement of stars and planets. As Deepak Chopra says, your biochemical rhythms are a symphony of the cosmos. Your cells are made up of atoms and inside atoms there are electrons, protons, quarks and gluons. Inside these, there is absolutely nothing you can see or put your finger on. But it isn't 'space', it's your consciousness – your mind and soul. I believe that consciousness is your connection to the universe.

In his theory of relativity, Albert Einstein taught that there was no real difference between matter and energy. They really are different forms of the same thing. This means that everything you see and touch is connected to the universe. So whatever you want or would like to create in your life is already connected to you.

It also means we are all connected to one another. This can really influence how we look at another person. Criticizing or judging them could really just be showing us a weakness in ourselves. This is something to bear in mind as we take steps to create our future.

The Positive View

Taking a positive view can really help us along the way. It can do so much for us on all levels. It is proven that having a more positive approach to life can enhance the longevity of our body, for a start.

Angels say that taking a positive view doesn't have to be about hugging trees (as good as that is) or constantly complimenting other people; it's about seeing things in a better light and recognizing that everything is perfect and is exactly what we created.

Our thoughts are so powerful, but we may not realize this; in fact, we probably don't even realize *what* we're thinking half the time. So one of the challenges in creating a better life is becoming more aware of what we are thinking about.

Angels have taught me an easy way to measure my thoughts. This is so useful because, as you'll probably agree, sometimes it can be difficult to be aware of what you're specifically thinking about. The trick to noticing what you are thinking is in your feelings, your emotions. Kamael says:

> *When you are low and are drawn in by negativity, you attract it more. So, if you recognize when you feel that way, you can seize the opportunity to change it. By consciously becoming positive, and releasing your fears and worries through crying, voicing your opinion and being assertive, you create space for positivity. Then, when you emit a positive frequency through your feelings, you attract more positive frequencies into your life, through abundance, a loving relationship, good health and a fulfilling career.*

As you adjust the way you think, the most amazing things will begin to happen: you will create miracles and begin to find the happiness and love you are searching for inside yourself.

Where There's a Will, There's a Way

We all know the effect feelings can have, because there's nothing worse than being around someone who's in a foul mood, is there? We also all know how brilliant it is when someone comes in with a positive vibe and in high spirits. At some point we've all been one or other of these people.

We can influence others with our feelings without even knowing. In smaller groups particularly, we can change the whole group energy just by how we feel, although it is said that those who are more contented within themselves are less easily affected by those around them.

In turn, we can be influenced too, of course. Have you been complaining recently about a friend or colleague's attitude? Do you find them draining or do they affect you more than you'd like? Remember that everything we say and do is a reflection of our inner self. So, when we judge or complain, we're only pointing out something we don't like about ourselves.

Complaining will also get us absolutely nowhere. Instead, we should take a non-interference approach. This is a Buddhist concept whereby we allow someone to learn their own lessons without having to tell them about it!

Changing Our Environment with Positive Thoughts

Instead of letting someone's negativity bring you down, why not take back your power and send loving thoughts out into the room?

You could say: 'Thank you, angels, for surrounding this room with your loving energy. Thank you for removing any energies which don't serve my purpose.'

Doing this will fill the room with nice energy – just watch the atmosphere lift!

You can also adapt this in your own way. One of my favourites comes from a nursery nurse who stands outside the nursery door every morning and tells all the people who walk through the door to imagine all their cares and worries being washed off by big sponges just as if they were at a carwash.

Remarkably, she finds that her nursery has very little sickness and is a positive space that even adults love to visit. Why not try this at your home or workplace?

The Universal Laws

Finally, I would like to take this opportunity to share with you my guide to the universal laws so you can learn to access love and abundance with the loving support of your guardian angel.

The universal laws are what it says on the tin – laws that define the way our universe works. Whether you're aware of them or not, they still affect you. They also affect angels. Through becoming more aware of them, you can become more positive and create a better life for yourself.

There are some laws you will already be aware of, such as karma – expressed in the old phrase 'What goes around comes around.' According to this law, whatever you put out to the world can be brought back to you. So, if you're consistently moaning and groaning, whining that everything is wrong and your life is rubbish, karma will keep bringing that back around to you and you'll find that the world is exactly what you keep saying it is. Think first!

There are three main universal laws that I work with constantly. They help me to remain aware of my thoughts and actions, and they can help you too.

1. The Law of Free Will

This law teaches that no matter what is thrown at us in life, we have the choice of how to react. We can allow ourselves to be drawn in by the negativity of a situation or we can transcend it entirely.

All of us have sometimes overreacted and got angry and frustrated with different situations and people in our life. We've all said, 'I should have done this' or 'I could have done that...' That way of thinking achieves nothing. The universe teaches us that everything is perfect and if something is supposed to happen, it will.

The aim with the Law of Free Will is to react compassionately to all situations and detach from all negativity. We can all do this, one step at a time.

It is important to think before reacting to anything in life. The universe teaches us that if we become frustrated or angry, we'll still have to learn a lesson. If we react with compassion and perform an act of non-interference, we're on the road to self-mastery. Self-mastery is the point in life when we're completely at peace with ourselves. Everything internal is in place, nothing external will affect us negatively – everything is perfect.

The Law of Free Will is also brought into play when it comes to asking a higher power for assistance. This higher power could be a saint, angel or deity to whom we wish to pray. These beings are unable to help us unless *we* ask. We have the choice.

2. The Law of Attraction

Most people will have heard of this law, but not everyone will have grasped the way it works. It teaches that whatever we put out to the universe will be attracted back towards us.

This means that if you approach life from a negative perspective, it's highly likely that you'll attract negative experiences back to you: things won't go to plan or you'll be unhappy. If you are loving, upbeat and positive, however, the Law of Attraction will bring loving, upbeat and positive experiences into your life.

The Law of Attraction can be used consciously to bring situations and things into our life that we need. These can include friends, relationships, physical or material items and happiness, but beware – this law has a very distinctive way of working. It's like this: if you want something, the universe will allow you to continue wanting it. If you feel that you don't deserve something but you still want it, the universe will keep you wanting it too. If you believe you already have it and bring that energy into your whole being, the universe will deliver it to you.

Here's an example. If you say, 'I want a new car, I want a new car, I want a new car,' over and over again, what will happen? It's highly likely that months will go by and you won't get a new car. But if you say, 'I welcome a new car into my life, I'm open to receiving and deserving of this new vehicle in my life, thank you, universe,' and you learn to believe this is true, then the universe will deliver.

Another way this universal law works is when you ask your angels for help. If you beg, ask for the same thing over again and are afraid that they won't help you, then you'll get stuck. One of my clients kept screaming every night, 'Why aren't my angels helping me?' She was so frustrated and lost because she wholeheartedly believed in their energy. But the universe basically heard, 'Angels not helping me,' and ensured it didn't happen.

The universe isn't bad or against us, it's completely neutral; we just have to learn how to work with it. When I told this client to say, 'Thank you, universe and angels, for constantly filling my life with blessings,' her whole life picked up. It's as easy as a few words and a change of perception.

Changing your beliefs can be difficult or easy. You have complete free will over how you feel, how you react and what you put out to the universe, so why not make it easy for yourself?

3: The Law of Manifestation

This law is similar to the Law of Attraction. However, manifesting something means that you're creating the energy yourself rather than attracting it to you. For example, instead of *attracting* positive experiences into your life, you're actually *creating* them.

So, if you're unhappy in life or with a certain situation, you can work with the Law of Manifestation to manifest changes. The best way to do this is through creative visualization. Don't worry about it or think you can't do it – you've done it many times without realizing! For example, you've been worried about a situation. Your imagination has run riot and you've seen everything going wrong. Then in reality things have gone wrong and it has been a horrible experience. And you just *knew* that was going to happen. Of course you did – you created it!

Instead of bringing these negative situations on yourself, you could change your thoughts and beliefs and manifest a positive experience for yourself. You could imagine everything going well, everyone being helpful and everything being perfect. Then you could just sit back and watch the magic happen!

Affirmations and the 'I Am'

An affirmation is a declaration that something is true. You can use affirmations to help create positive experiences in your life. As we have already seen, saying 'I am...' attracts that energy to you. When you say it, the universe believes you. It will help other people believe you too.

Your affirmations can affect others as well. If you continually say something about someone, you're putting those beliefs out to the universe and the Law of Attraction will make them true for you. So, for example, if you say, 'He just doesn't communicate,' or, 'She just doesn't love me,' that person will behave that way even more towards you.

Instead of sending out these negative affirmations, you could affirm – and believe – differently by saying, 'I am surrounded by open and communicative people,' or, 'I am open to receiving love in my life.' You'll be astounded by the results.

You've Got to Mean It!

One important thing to remember here is that if you say something but believe something else, the universe will go with the thing you believe. If, on the other hand, you can believe what you're saying and see it in your mind at the same time, then the universe will make it true for you.

This isn't always easy, of course. We all have a tendency towards negative thinking from time to time, but negative thoughts can be turned into positive ones very easily – and then you just have to believe them!

- Instead of saying, 'My body is ugly,' try, 'I am perfect just the way I am.'
- Instead of saying, 'No one loves me,' try, 'I love myself and I am loved and accepted by others.'
- Instead of saying, 'I'm just not good enough,' try, 'I am always seen for who I truly am – positive and loving.'
- Instead of saying, 'I never have enough money,' try, 'I am abundant and comfortable, my finances support me and I am safe.'
- Instead of saying, 'I'm so angry all the time,' try, 'I am calm and collected. Nothing can remove me from this space of peace.'

The Archangel of the Universal Laws

There is an archangel who governs the universal laws. When you're working with these laws – and, of course, learning them – you can call on him for help. His name is Archangel

Raziel, a name which means 'Secrets of God'. That's exactly what these laws are – they are secrets which I'm now sharing with you.

I've always seen Raziel in a golden light. His skin is dark in my mind; he almost looks Egyptian. His energy is wise and knowing and you can call him into your space while learning this work.

All you have to do is imagine yourself covered in a golden shimmering light and say: 'Thank you, Archangel Raziel, for surrounding me in your wise light. Thank you for helping me learn the universal laws and teach me how to apply them to my life. And so it is.'

The Path to Happiness

It is possible to find happiness in everything you do. If you follow my four simple steps, with the help of the angels your world will change beyond your wildest dreams:

- First, you must *let go*. You have to let go of all that you no longer need in your life. Let go of what is no longer right for you. Listen to what your gut is telling you. Be willing to change.
- Secondly, you must *forgive*. You have to forgive others and, ultimately, yourself. Holding a grudge against yourself means that you're not in control, and holding a grudge against someone else basically hands them your power. Remember you have free will over how you react.
- Thirdly, you have to *approve of yourself*. See yourself in a positive light. Always try your best and recognize you're

always doing the best you can. You can choose how you see yourself – choose the best view.

- Finally, *create new things and change your life*. Stop following old patterns. Be open to new experiences and change what you feel you no longer need in your life. Create and attract new experiences using the universal laws.

The Art of Letting Go

Letting go is essential for us to move forwards in life. If we consistently hold on to things we no longer have a use for, we allow the energy of that situation to surround us and hold us back.

For example, if you've had a relationship where things have gone wrong but you've managed to reunite through love, this is good. However, if you still think of the past or hold on to the negativity of that situation, harking back to the bad times, it will only end badly. Holding on to something so deeply can be one of the biggest causes of it repeating.

You could also have it in your mind that something negative is going to happen to you. One of the situations that I always encourage people to let go of is when they say, 'I think I'm going to die young.' Please don't do that. The Law of Attraction always delivers – don't hand your life away!

Finally, yet again, affirmations can be very powerful. Daily, you can say: 'I'm willing to release old patterns' and 'I release and let go of anything standing in the way of my happiness' and 'I welcome new experiences.'

The Art of Forgiveness

Forgiveness is a very difficult process, but it's something we all have to do – especially if the person or situation is still in our life or we need to forgive ourselves.

Not forgiving someone, or playing the blame game, is basically handing our power over to someone else. It can create resentment, which has been scientifically proven to be one of the main mentally generated causes of cancer.

Forgiveness is easier said than done, of course. Many clients I've worked with have felt the need to get rid of anger before they can forgive, so I've developed some tips to help with that process:

- Get anger and resentment out of your system by punching something (not someone!) Find a quiet, safe and undisturbed space and scream and shout as much as you like as you punch a pillow or cushion or beanbag. Grind your teeth if you want; shout and swear if you need to. Do it as much as you can – you need to let the anger out in order to move on and create happiness in your life.

- Go to the top of a big hill and scream as many times as you want. You may even wish to scream the name of a person or company you're ready to let go of.

Once you've let go of your anger, you must work on forgiveness. There are two options when it comes to forgiveness: you can make it difficult or easy. I always choose the easiest route possible! I aim to take the bull by the horns, say my piece and get things off my chest and then do my best to make peace with a situation.

If you find it difficult to forgive someone, that's great! Resistance towards something really shows it needs to be done, and just by becoming aware of that, you're a step closer to inner happiness.

Things happen. That's just the way it is! You can learn from them and move on or carry them around and let them drag you down. Tell yourself you're ready to move on and ready for the new. Repeat this every time a negative thought comes into your head.

You can also bring about forgiveness through communication. You may actually have to reach closure with someone by having a conversation and telling them that you're ready to forgive. It might take courage, but it'll be worth it.

For self-forgiveness, you could go to the mirror and look yourself directly in the eye and say: 'I forgive you. Now let's move on from here – it's time for positivity!'

You can also bring about forgiveness through visualization. If you're unable to see the person again or would prefer not to, you could imagine speaking to them and telling them that you forgive them. You could do this for yourself too – imagine telling yourself that you're forgiven. It will work just as well as looking at yourself in the mirror!

Another good way to forgive someone is imagine them on a stage and send them loads of good vibes. Surround them in positive light and energy and you'll feel better for it.

Louise Hay says a great way to forgive is through affirmations. All we have to do is look in the mirror and say: 'I forgive and I am forgiven.' When we can truly believe these words and look at ourselves in the eye as we say them, we will be released.

There's an amazing archangel named Zadkiel whose name means 'The righteousness of God'. Zadkiel works with an energy called the violet flame. This is a space or retreat we can visit in our mind through prayer and meditation. The violet flame allows us to put all burdens, anger and unforgiven situations onto its beautiful embers so we release all our unnecessary baggage to the universe in love.

Call in Archangel Zadkiel to help you release and forgive at this time by saying: 'Zadkiel, thank you for surrounding me in your violet light. I now forgive and I am forgiven for all acts and situations that hold me back. Using the power of the violet flame, I release all that I no longer need. I am the violet flame. I am free!'

Approve of Yourself

Have you ever met someone who moans and groans about everyone around them? If so, then it's really a reflection of how they feel inside. If you judge people around you all the time, it shows that you're looking for errors in others because you really don't like yourself.

If you want to find happiness, you must stop being overly critical of both yourself and of others and learn to approve of yourself.

This couldn't be easier. It's fun too. I should know: every time I finish a show or a reading with a client, I tell myself I did absolutely brilliantly – and I mean it. If you put your heart and soul into what you love, why should you constantly pick at yourself for it?

Approve of yourself, realize you're a good person who's doing their best, and if you've had your bad moments, don't put yourself down but be willing to change things in the future. You've let go, you've forgiven yourself and others, and now you approve of yourself too – you're on the path to happiness!

Use this affirmation: 'I approve of myself and accept only the best for myself in life.'

As We Pass Through

I do hope that you've enjoyed all that we've shared in this book, and learned from it too, and that your own spiritual talent has been nurtured and developed.

It has been an emotional journey for me and I feel such love for my beloved nana who started me on this path. I am so grateful to her and am committed to ensuring her memory is honoured through the work I do and will continue to do, and I hope I will meet you again as I do so.

At a time of uncertainty and doubt in our world, it is comforting to know that there are forces that work solely for our good, no matter what. I feel honoured to act as a guide to them.

Please do take a moment every day to connect with your own angels in the ways I've suggested. I hope that you all receive love and support from these wonderful beings who care so deeply for us all.

Until we meet again...

ACKNOWLEDGEMENTS

Thank you angels for making all of this possible! There has been so much loving support in my life to share this work.

Thank you Mum for running the back end of our business and for giving me those kicks in the butt I need. I am a professional dreamer and for that reason I need someone like you to keep me directed and focused. Thanks for your love, your incredible food and your acceptance.

Thanks Dad for reminding me that there's more to life than work, and to have fun. I'm grateful for your love and acceptance.

Special thanks to The Angel Club for all of your support and encouragement. It started as a small group of 14 people and now we have 150 people gathering twice a month and over 2,000 members online who celebrate the angels with me.

Thanks to all of the amazing people at Hay House UK: Michelle Pilley – my commissioning editor who likes to connect at a soul level. She gets the energy thing and helps me shine brighter.

Ruth Tewkesbury, Jo Burgess and Jessica Gibson – thanks for keeping me in the media, on the stage and looking after my wellbeing while we do all of it.

Extending my thanks to the editorial team at Hay House UK, especially Julie Oughton, and Leanne Siu Anastasi for designing the cover.

Thanks to my brother from another mother – Drew Barnes – for the cover photo.

Thank you everyone who let me share their life and their story. It's been truly enlightening. I am grateful to be here.

ABOUT THE AUTHOR

Drew John Barnes

Kyle Gray has had spiritual encounters from an early age. When he was just four years old, his grandmother's soul visited him from beyond the grave.

Growing up, Kyle always had an ability to hear, feel and see what goes beyond the natural senses, which eventually led him to discovering the power and love of angels in his teens.

Now, at just 27, Kyle is one of the most hip and sought-after experts in his field. With his unique ability to stay grounded and keep it real, he re-introduces the idea of angels in a modern and accessible way. Kyle's talks in the UK and around Europe sell out within days, and his private sessions have a two-year waiting list. He is the author of four books.

www.kylegray.co.uk

THE Certified Card Reader ONLINE COURSE

MASTER ORACLE & TAROT READING

with Colette Baron-Reid, Kyle Gray, Rev. Sharon Anne Klingler, Denise Linn, Sandra Anne Taylor, and Radleigh Valentine

Have you always wanted to learn to read oracle and tarot cards? Or do you want to take your card-reading skills through the roof? Have you ever considered becoming a certified professional card reader and sharing your gifts with the world?

If you have, this is your chance to learn everything you need to know about card reading—**PLUS get certified!**

In this premiere online course, six world-renowned teachers team up to bring you a certification program like none other. Whether you're a total newbie or an experienced card reader, they'll teach you everything you need to know to **master the mystical art of card reading** and—if you so choose—create a fulfilling spiritual business.

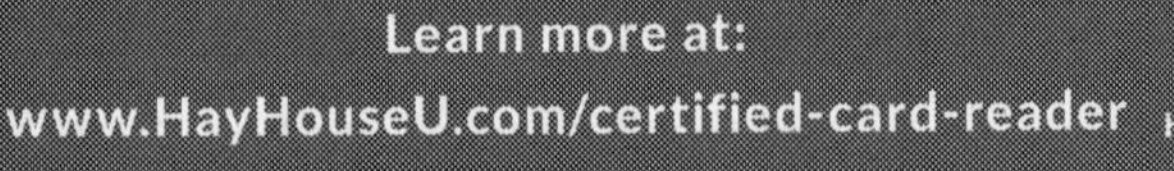

Printed in the United States
By Bookmasters